Touching the World through Reiki

Eileen Dey, MA, LMHC

BOOK PUBLISHERS NETWORK

Book Publishers Network
P.O. Box 2256
Bothell • WA • 98041
Ph • 425-483-3040
www.bookpublishersnetwork.com

10 9 8 7 6 5 4 3 2 1

Printed in the United States of America

LCCN 2010934503
ISBN10 1-935359-52-5
ISBN13 978-1-935359-52-4

All client and student names and circumstances have been changed to protect their confidentiality.

Editor: Julie Scandora
Cover designer: Laura Zugzda
Typographer: Stephanie Martindale

Before the beginning of great brilliance, there must be chaos. Before a brilliant person begins something great, they must look foolish to the crowd.

I-Ching

Reiki says:
Believe in your self and your abilities
Trust your intuition
Be compassionate to others
Let go of limiting beliefs
Honor the pause
Make space for healing
Give yourself permission to receive
Be prepared to be surprised

Contents

Acknowledgements

This book has been in the making since I began my journey in creating the Reiki Training Program back in 2003. I am indebted to all the many hundreds of Reiki students who have taught me so much through each class, and I have been honored to witness how each of them has brought Reiki into the world.

Special gratitude to the preliminary writing of "Making Space for Healing" with Andrea Rae. Thanks for all those hours of brainstorming and creating the initial space to get me finally to write!

Thank you to:

Julie Scandora for her patience and creativity in guiding me through the editing process!

My friend and mentor Karma Llundup for providing me with a framework and launching pad for my Insight Reiki method to develop.

My friend and colleague Michael Emanuel, who helped to nurture the Reiki for Veterans program and continues to be a guiding force in its development.

Tom Brophy for his support, encouragement, and witnessing all these years. Jen Yost for her sage advice and her commitment to the spiritual path. Samantha Parrott for her infectious spirit of light.

The wise women council of NAIT for holding space not only for my clients' but also for my own soul growth and development. Hilary Bolles and Shelly Shelly for bearing witness to all my "processes"!

The past Reiki Soundscape crew who taught me what having a "happening" was all about.

The Reiki communities in New Jersey, Philadelphia, and Seattle who helped shape who I am and what I do. My Reiki masters Cherie Wine-Prashun and Alena Huble and my professors in graduate school and troupe at IAM-Boeing, who nurtured the emerging counselor within.

The amazing individuals who have been and who are the Reiki Fellowship and to everyone who comes and is coming to the Reiki circles and clinics at East West Bookshop!

William Lee Rand and *Reiki News* magazine for publishing the articles included in this book.

All my Artist Way groups, which have kept the creative muse spirit alive!

My acting coaches and colleagues who give me another outlet to shine!

My grandparents Ed and Agnes, Martin and Johanna, who believed and loved my creative nature. To the Van Vliets and the Wursts in my family who love and support me even if they aren't sure what Reiki is about!

My parents, Marty and Dorise Wurst, who provided me with so many opportunities throughout my life that I have been able to complete this book.

To my Reiki cats Blackie, Middie, Kai, Comet, and Suki—angels in fur, both in life and beyond!

And lastly, to Richard Scott Schilling, whose devoted love and belief in my ability as a healer, leader, and visionary has helped me in completing this first (of many) written works.

Love to you all!

Introduction

Over 6.8 billion people inhabit this vast world, and in my travels, I have come to realize that even as many cultural differences separate us, many similarities bring us together, including a desire for love, happiness, and within that, peace.

Reiki as a means for healing and transformation offers such a means for achieving peace—world peace.

I have taught groups where each student adhered to a different faith, religion, or political party and yet could all come together to work as a healing unit without discord. Reiki, being Universal Energy, does not discriminate. It is here for all of us: human, animal, plant, planet.

By learning to work with it on ourselves and others, we become our own vehicles for compassion. Cultivating compassion allows us to spread world peace and in effect 'touch the world through Reiki'.

There are many Reiki how-to and historical manuals, but this is not one of them. *Touching the world through Reiki* serves as inspiration to those who have already taken or are contemplating taking a Reiki class.

This is about my own personal journey on the Reiki path as I worked with and trained other Reiki practitioners and the possibility of touching the world with Reiki through one's commitment to the path. Through the development of my training program, we have taught over a thousand students from twenty countries.

I have found five tools that work incredibly well in helping the Reiki practitioner or student succeed on his or her path, and provide insight and wisdom along the way. Each tool I present has served as a guide for my clients, students, and my own Reiki healing. By utilizing each one, an individual's worldview can expand, thus enabling him or her to connect with fellow humans and begin to understand the work he or she has come here to do. The tools also offer practitioners and masters ways in which they can enhance their own work in the world.

In addition, I offer various mainstream applications for Reiki practitioners to explore as possible starting points for their work as well as ideas on where to apply Reiki, such as in hospitals, for animals, and integrated in various professions.

But these chapters are merely a suggestion, a place to start. If they call to you, then use them as a model.

Whether you want to practice on yourself or your family or consider Reiki as a vocational path, this book is for you—to reflect, receive, and add to your continued learning.

What is Reiki?

R eiki (pronounced RAY-kee) is a Japanese form of hands-on healing. It was rediscovered as a healing art in the nineteenth century by a man named Mikao Usui, who, through passing the tradition down through his students, enabled them to bring Reiki to the United States in the last part of the twentieth century. I refer the reader to the bibliography for some of the many books that provide more information about the origins of Reiki.

Reiki is ancient—it's always been a part of the Earth although other cultures have called it different names—and it has evolved as we have evolved. It used to be taught as part of Buddhist philosophy, but the healing applications were discarded in favor of the spiritual tenets instead.

Reiki comes from "rei," meaning universal, and "ki," meaning energy, and together means Universal Energy. In practicing Reiki on oneself or in receiving a Reiki treatment, one is basking in the healing light in a safe and healing manner, permitting the release of any debris or blocks (physical, mental, or emotional) that might be occurring in the body.

One becomes "attuned" to Reiki through an initiation by one's Reiki master (teacher). During the initiation, the teacher facilitates the student's re-awakening to the flow of Universal Energy through facilitating the expansion of the student's own aura or electromagnetic field. Sacred Reiki symbols are also visualized within the field, re-establishing the connection the student has to healing and to his or her own true potential.

Reiki stimulates the immune system response, similar to acupuncture in that it flows through the meridians, which are energy pathways that traverse the whole body. It soothes the nerves and calms the mind. Practicing Reiki and meditation every day gives you a focus for the day and over time can guide you in other parts of your life.

Reiki stimulates the body to return to the natural state of flow and ease. It is a gentle method, portable in its preventative action. All one needs is to learn the method.

Diving In

I n my practicing and working with the Universal Energy of Reiki for over fifteen years, I've come to understand this connection to flow and ease. And in the process of recently completing my scuba diving certification, I tangibly experienced what I've come to embody as a Reiki practitioner and teacher. Let me help you understand.

Floating through the infinite expanse of the ocean, you imagine what you want to create. Think of starfish; a starfish appears. Watch your bubbles cascade upwards; you see physics in action. Sink to the bottom of the sea floor; you experience gravity that affects all the earth, everything. Watching a starfish engulfing a clam, you see the process of living and dying in front of your eyes.

Reiki is like this circle of life, ever present, permeating all of the world. We need to create the space and place to dive in and experience this phenomenon. When we—those of us practicing Reiki, regardless of our place on the experience spectrum—gather, we all create a field of potential, channeling our unified energy into a space of intention. The intention lifts the vibration of all who are present, raising consciousness and allowing for a transcendence of physical and mental limitations.

Like the scuba diver, you become neutrally buoyant in a sea of healing energy. What does not serve you can leave, falling away effortlessly. What is true to your essence remains. That is the heart of Reiki. It leads you to the place you were meant to be. What do you want to manifest? Working with the energy of Reiki allows you to attract and be attracted to that which is of the highest good.

But it is not a manipulative energy. Like the ocean, it just is. You can't force the ocean! Universal Energy has no boundaries, only infinite potential. Likewise, we have our own inner and outer space. This vast expanse is our true realm. The physical, three-dimensional realm in which we spend our lives on Earth represents only one view. Dive deep into the oceans, cast out into the stars. These places are not just physical manifestations; they also exist within the soul of each and every one of us, all around the world. When we take this journey, we transcend our boundaries. We become aware that we are ONE—one planet, one world. We are not our ego identities. We are not our personalities … These are colors of the rainbow each and every one of us represents at any given point in time.

You can use the wetsuit as the analogy of our ego. It allows one to travel, function, and survive through the matrix of the water environment. It's a covering, a protection, and a container. It keeps one's physical body intact. Yet, the wetsuit only works when you let some water (ki) into it. As that water coats your body, the insulating layer of the suit allows the water to heat to your body temperature. But when it comes down to it, the wetsuit/ego is only one layer on top of the layer of water on top of our physical body, which is basically a bag of water contained by a layer of skin.

When we remove all those layers, those preconceptions, we are exposed and engulfed by the sea of ki, of Reiki, of the Universe.

But unlike being in water, where if we were to remove the wetsuit we would be in peril, when we move the ego aside in the air, on the land, we merge with the ki that comes from each and every one of us, from all the plants, the grass, the trees, the flowers, the water around us.

Let yourself go, feel the force of the energy present in this world, the nature, the people, the intention. Reiki is about getting out of the way and making space for healing to occur. Healing means becoming whole. We come into attunement, at oneness with our true essence, and in effect, connecting with this world, touching all of creation. Reiki practitioners and masters (teachers) serve as guides on this path back to source. We are your scuba instructors. Take the dive, journey and return transformed.

The preceding comes from my speech at The One Gathering (www.theonegathering.com), an annual event in Seattle, Washington.

Exercise

A. Feeling the Reiki Flow

Reiki energy is all around us, and we are able to tap into it. I do recommend taking a workshop because your own ability to hold space for the healing potential is strengthened and you learn basics of working with others and yourself. You also receive attunements to the energy, which mean "becoming at one." It is a sacred blessing meditation that connects you to the lineage of Reiki, the previous teachers, so that when you practice, you are supported in your work and "in tune" with the vibration of those teachings.

Now, let's just see what you perceive when you hold space for this healing energy.

Come with a very curious mind. Just open your thinking, keeping a question such as, "What will happen when I do this?" in front of you while holding no expectations for the results. Let yourself get comfortable, either lying down or sitting in a relaxed position.

1. Begin to visualize your own connection to heaven and earth.

2. See, feel, and imagine a flow of energy or water from the Universe through you to the earth and vice versa.

3. This energy is greater than you. It flows through you. You act only as a humble conduit.

4. Give yourself a few moments, connecting to that idea, to that flow as you effortlessly let the energy continue through you.

5. Then, ever so lightly, place your hands a few inches apart in front of you, palms facing.

6. Remain curious, not forcing, just being.

7. Rest lightly, breathing in and out. Reiki is an offering and never forces.

8. Then move your hands about a foot apart from each other. Notice what you notice.

9. Still just being, force nothing, effortless.

10. Perhaps you notice the energy flowing through you, perhaps there is a sensation of warmth or tingling, perhaps nothing. Just treat whatever you notice curiously, without effort.

11. Now move your hands two feet apart.

12. Breathe into that space.

13. Bring the palms back together, not touching. Relax and remember to breathe. Wondrous. Inhale.

14. Shake your palms out and notice what you feel now.

Part 1
My Journey to the Reiki Path and 5 Tools to Transform Your World

I loved the process of discovering the Reiki path and meeting people around the world through this journey. It started initially by exploring the bodywork technique of Polarity Therapy.

At the age of twenty-four, after having worked as a social worker for several years, I was realizing the energetic nature of healing that occurred in my counseling sessions with clients, something beyond diagnoses and systematic treatment.

I took a class in Polarity on a whim. It talked about chakra and meridian systems. I had heard of these concepts earlier in my life, having grown up with a mom who had exposed me to the New Age ideas of Edgar Cayce, dreams, and holistic healing. But I had always thought of these ideas more as philosophies than practical applications. Then, once I was out in the working world, interacting with people, I began to gain a glimpse of their relevance to the physical.

So, Polarity caught my eye, and I diligently would take the hour bus ride from suburban New Jersey, where I had grown up, into the bustling metropolis of Manhattan, down into Greenwich Village to study at the only holistic center available to me at the time, the Open Center.

I'll never forget lying on a massage table for the first time and having a caring practitioner put her hands under my head. Radiant energy flowed into my body, and I felt such love and support. I felt at home. Each class taught me aspects of the Ayurvedic system of healing, the doshas, or types of constitution that makes up each of us, and the honor of touching others with my hands to facilitate energy balancing and a return to harmony.

I would have continued on through Polarity, but I kept noticing I was trying to figure out how energy healing worked. How was I making that happen? One day, a colleague of mine in class noticed how hard I was trying. He said perhaps I might want to look into the system of Reiki for another approach.

It was the first time I had heard that word, yet it, like the experience of lying on the table for the first time, resonated in me as if I had returned home.

So, I began to look for where I might study Reiki.

This was before the Internet made Google searching possible or even the Yellow Pages had listings of Reiki. So, I just kept out an antenna for this word, and one day, as I was sitting in a Laundromat, of all places, I saw a holistic guide of therapies lying on the table. When I opened it, the page read "Reiki" and listed the phone number of the woman who was to become my teacher.

I called her, Cherie Wine-Prashun, and asked about this kind of work. She explained the concept of Universal Energy and being a channel and invited me to her home where she was holding a Reiki practice session, called a "Reiki share," the next week.

When I arrived at her very ordinary looking suburban home, I had the distinct impression that, although Reiki sounded magical and foreign, it also seemed to be something that could fit into the normal world. To confirm this observation, Cherie opened the door, looking more like Florence Henderson as Mrs. Brady on the *Brady Bunch* TV show than some guru in flowing robes with a turban.

She led me down into her converted basement rec room that had about twenty people in groups of four, circled around four different massage tables. On each table, a person was lying down while the others around had their hands on or gently above them. I watched in wonder and awe for the first half hour or so.

No one seemed to be "doing" anything. In contrast, in Polarity, we had all remained conscious of what sides of the body we were working on and how we were manipulating energy. But these people were just resting their hands in one place for many minutes at a time.

After several rounds of people had received their treatments, Cherie advised me to lie down on a table as well. I was nervous because I had never experienced four people and their eight hands lying on me, but I settled in as best as I could, took a deep breath, and within the first minute, I felt myself gently taken away to the meditative place I often experienced in deep meditation. I then felt my mind and body smooth out, my consciousness expand, and any worries disappear. I felt as if I stayed on that table for hours, but when the circle told me it was time to get up, I realized I had been lying down only for about fifteen minutes.

I got off and walked over to the side of the room, sitting down, astonished by the experience. This was truly magical, yet everyone and the whole environment looked completely ordinary. At that moment, I knew I was truly hooked to pursue the Reiki path.

Several weeks later, I took my first Level 1 workshop and began to learn how to perform a Reiki treatment on myself and others. I learned of its Japanese origins by the founder of the system, Mikao Usui, its philosophy, and the personal experiences of everyone in the group.

I experienced how profound Reiki could work on others was when my kitten somehow managed to get sandwiched between my screen door and the front door. When I shut the door, not knowing his predicament, I ended up squashing his little foot with a resulting loud MEOW. I immediately opened the door and found him pitifully limping. I inspected the foot but noticed it still could flex normally and that my kitten was more stunned than anything.

Nevertheless, I went to bed shortly after, and to my surprise, the kitten lay on my pillow with his paw outstretched. I placed my hand over his paw, giving him Reiki, and slept with him practically the whole night (something he never did before or has done since). In the morning he bounded about as if nothing had happened.

During this early learning period, I would frequently encounter circumstances in which immediate attention (in the healing direction) was needed. Having only Reiki with me, I would apply it, to myself, my partner, my family, my cats, etc. and begin to see the delicate effect of relaxation, calmness and sometimes serenity that would occur. At first I attributed the changes to coincidence, but I soon came to understand the transformative power of Reiki at work.

Several more weeks after my initial workshop, I returned and began my true Reiki education: attending Reiki shares (or circles, as they are also known) each week for the next year.

I interacted with a different group of people each week—sometimes upwards of twenty people at one time. Many were from New Jersey, but we started to attract international visitors from Egypt, France, Spain, and Mexico. I began to see how Reiki as a practice was also a universal language.

As the months passed and I went through the subsequent levels of Reiki training, my life began changing around me. I left the relationship I was in that was not honoring me. I immersed myself more fully in graduate school to complete a master's degree in counseling. And I moved into my own apartment for the first time in my life.

By the end of the year, I had bought my first Reiki table through William Lee Rand's The International Center for Reiki Training. At that point, I knew I wanted to become a Reiki Master and integrate Reiki teachings into my counseling practice. I didn't know what that would look like because I had never met a counselor who incorporated energy healing into his or her work, but the idea kept calling me, and I was listening.

After receiving my Reiki Master and master's degree in counseling in the same year, I moved into the city of brotherly love, Philadelphia. There I began the path of developing my own Reiki practice, teaching my first classes, and holding my own Reiki circles. I met other Reiki Masters who encouraged me to incorporate sound healing into my work, to be a public speaker for Reiki, and to become the teacher I am today.

After two years of living in the urban sprawl, I began feeling I needed to move to another place to continue this work. I was still having my counseling and Reiki practices in separate spheres, but I wanted an integration of the two and an environment that would encourage me to pursue my dream.

During this time of wanting to move on, I attended a workshop on holistic career counseling. The speaker led us through many different exercises, and in one intense meditation session, I had a very strong vision—

MOVE TO SEATTLE!

When I closed my eyes, I saw the Olympic Mountains and Puget Sound as if I were staring from the Port of Seattle. I had to trust the vision. Even though I didn't know what "move to Seattle" meant, I felt I had to hold the space for it.

Within only a month of applying to different jobs in the Northwest, I had gotten an interview and then been offered a job! The move was one of the easiest and freest flowing I have ever encountered. By now I was becoming convinced that the more I trusted my intuition, allowed room for Reiki, and gave myself permission to receive, the more I was living in line with my true path, and the easier my life became.

I sold most of my belongings back East, asked my boyfriend at the time to join me, and moved out to the Pacific Northwest. I was thirty years old.

As I began my job in corporate America, counseling clients who were getting laid off, I realized the integration of my work was beginning to happen as I found myself offering Reiki in each session. When I added the application of Reiki to the session, my clients began having breakthroughs, and they wanted to learn how to do Reiki for themselves. And so I began the foundation for the Reiki Training Program (RTP) and the technique of Insight Reiki I later developed and offer as Tool #3.

RTP eventually became a healing arts vocational school licensed by Washington State to provide Reiki classes, sessions, and practice circles. And if students wanted to go further in their education, there were two options to provide practitioner and teacher training.

Over the next ten years, I nurtured the school, teaching over a thousand students and bringing classes into community colleges, the University of Washington, and holistic centers as well as establishing my own healing center.

RTP had graduated enough alumni to create its own outreach organization, called The Reiki Fellowship. Through the Fellowship, we've been able to take Reiki on the road to expos, fairs, into corporate America, to veterans, to open another branch of the school in Eastern Washington, and our latest endeavor, to help heal the most polluted river in Seattle, the Duwamish.

Getting involved in acting school introduced me to a whole new world of media as well as bringing Reiki onto the 'main stage'. In the process, I've recorded three guided meditation CD's to help my students and the next endeavor attempts to combine our outreach with Duwamish into a documentary film.

Someone who recently met me for the first time said, "When I think of Reiki in Seattle, I think of Eileen Dey." It has been quite an honor to be involved in the work I do.

My intention is to continue to reach out to the world through my work and to offer wisdom, guidance, and training to those interested in Reiki. I have come to realize that as I have moved through this process and assisted others in walking in Reiki that it is a path of abundance and creativity. Through Reiki, you come to trust that the Universe will support you in all you do. How can it not? You are acting as a channel for the greater good, so the support for what you do and how you build your practice will be there.

As you step onto that path, you will begin to interact with individuals from many different backgrounds, cultures, and belief systems. Your journey will be unique, just as you are, but it's important to have tools that can assist you as you traverse the landscape of energy work.

Through my own experience and witnessing of others, I have developed five tools to transform your world. They are: Discernment, Making Space and Time for the Journey, Insight Reiki, Cultivating the Creative Career, and Attending and Establishing Reiki Circles and Shares in Your Community. These tools and the exercises presented will expand your Reiki awareness and begin to create opportunities with you to touch the world through Reiki.

Sit back, enjoy, and have fun with this book. And may you receive countless blessings on your continued Reiki journey.

Tool #1:
Discernment in Navigating the Spiritual Path

dis.cern.ment *n.* The act or process of exhibiting
keen insight and good judgment.

Discernment is like having the lights on in a dark cave. It allows you to see and trust your inner vision. Each level of Reiki allows you to integrate greater levels of discernment or wisdom.

In traveling on your journey in connecting with others, discernment provides a context for interacting with all the variety of choices a practitioner has to face. You realize what relationships, people, and situations serve and honor you and what do not.

Discernment is cultivated by practicing Reiki on yourself and in the sessions where you receive a Reiki treatment. The more you connect with Universal Energy, the more you connect with your higher-wisdom self. In this realm of your being, you are able to exercise clarity of thought and mind. It's actually a mechanism that permits compassionate understanding of your world, and the various people and animals that inhabit it. Discernment serves as a guide for the work you were meant to do.

You can have the ability to meet others from a variety of backgrounds and see the truth of their situation, their issues, and how to assist in their healing. The same goes for your own personal development. You become your own torch-bearer of truth when it comes to making decisions and interacting with the world.

There are several points to discernment I feel are key to address:

1. Trust your feelings.
2. Exercise limits and boundaries.
3. Pay attention to coincidences.
4. Be curious.
5. Stick to one path until you have achieved some level of mastery.

1. Trust your feelings.

This is probably the most important to cultivate in oneself as a Reiki practitioner. Learn to pay attention to when your own body gives you the wisdom that something is true. When a client or student tells me something that is a profound truth, without doubt, the hairs on my arms stand up. I've realized this is my energy body's way of giving me additional information.

Discernment is using your own body and mind as an instrument of perception and insight. What is your way of experiencing profound truth? Energy shivers down your spine or on the top of your head? Hair standing on end? A knowing from within your gut? Take time to notice how your body responds when someone mentions a truth. Notice what your body does or doesn't do when someone isn't being true to his or her self.

As a practitioner, you are going to confront many situations that seem beyond the scope of your experience and practice. These are the growth hurdles you need to jump or cross in order to continue advancing onward in your practice and grow as a person. One such occurrence happened to me in my private practice where I could "feel" that my client was going to cry in the same way I "feel" the truth, and I thought, will I be able to handle this? I found out that, yes, this woman was going to cry, and she did with great convulsions, and yet I was feeling so very unprepared for this. I stood there, holding my hands over her heart and supporting her in her process. She told me afterwards that she never felt so relived of the issues in her relationships that had plagued her. After crying in this supportive atmosphere, she knew she could become more of herself. I felt the same. I had crossed a hurdle in my own process, and I, too, could be more myself, and I was in every session that occurred thereafter.

When you are more yourself or in your higher wisdom self, your clients, students, friends, and family find it easier to connect with you. Universality, in all senses of the word, permeates your presence. And the old adage, "like attracts like," comes into play the more you allow this higher wisdom through. You will align with others, circles of friends, colleagues, clients, and students who support the light that shines through you.

And you will be attracted to others and situations that honor that light. This may take you into the realm of working with Reiki to help the environment or to promote world peace or to bring this healing into organizational structures like healthcare.

Discernment as a tool creates a clearer vision of the path you are to trod in connecting with the world. It helps you select people for your inner circle who will support you. And throughout the whole process, it works with you as you hold true to yourself.

2. Exercise limits and boundaries.

This is another key component of discernment. As a helper, you will encounter people who require your assistance dealing with their own concerns, needs, desires. As the Buddhists say, "reality is suffering" ... and there is a lot of it in the world. Luckily, as a practitioner, you have a gift that can help many people.

But you will have to decide for yourself where to put your efforts, where to focus your intentions, whom to say yes to. Remember that a healthy functioning of the Reiki system encourages reciprocity, equal exchange, give and take.

For example, years ago, I met a Reiki practitioner, Celia. She had recently moved to town and wanted to connect with the Reiki community. During the first meeting, realized I would have to put certain boundaries up around her because she was pulling my own energy into her. She wanted to connect and have someone help her get her life straightened out as she struggled to recover from a relationship gone bad.

Celia mentioned that she was looking for a retreat center so I gave her the names of some of the ones I knew. She found one, and as she settled in, she seemed more at ease and invited me up to come stay. While I was there, we agreed to do a Reiki trade session with each other. During the whole time she was giving me Reiki, she talked all about *her* life and about what *she* was going to do in the future. I felt overwhelmed by her story and unable to ask her to stop her talking because I kept hoping she would come to an end of her discourse. After all, she was going to get her own session; this was my time to receive. I had the discernment to finish out the trade (giving her Reiki in silence because I needed it!) and then bowed out and left early.

The experience taught me to be more vocal before I receive a session, telling the practitioner what I need. It also heightened my discernment sense a bit on perceiving when clients and students are in a needy place and to support them but not to lend myself totally (as in the case of a trade) while they are in their process.

The important thing to remember is to be gentle with yourself when you feel your boundaries have been stretched. Consider these as detours on your path. You get to observe some interesting scenery you ordinarily would not have the chance to, and you always eventually return to your path.

In Reiki, we say, "That which does not serve (your higher self) falls away." With discernment, be prepared for relationships to change and shift. My relationship with Celia certainly did. I had to pull back, honoring my need for a stronger boundary with her while she went through her own transition.

On the flip side, by having stronger boundaries with myself and honoring my needs, I have drawn to me and been drawn to other practitioners where there is mutual support. I have a colleague, Angie, who has been integrating counseling and bodywork for many years. We met through a group that supports this work and have been giving and receiving session trades with each other for almost a decade. Our relationship is clear: we are colleagues with similar backgrounds. We meet for trades and in our professional group and support each other in our endeavors out in the community.

Healthy boundaries equal relationships that respect the individuals involved. Through respect comes trust in yourself and in your relationship to the world around you. You begin to trust the greater wisdom of the Universe when you have relationships that honor you. Establishing healthy limits permits the next facet of discernment, paying attention to coincidences, to take on meaning.

3. Pay attention to coincidences.

Cultivate a pattern of noticing coincidences. They often happen for a reason. For example, when I was feeling called to move to Seattle, I just noticed what drew my attention: job boards, groups, news items about that city. As I honed in on those items, I noticed job offers, Reiki groups, and other connections beginning to line up to help assist in that move. I've also found "paying attention with a certain intention" to be a helpful exercise for others to use to bring more serendipitous experiences into their lives. As you notice coincidences, you connect to others who support your work in the world.

I see coincidences as signposts from the Universe, and we welcome their wondrous results into our lives when we let go of having to produce a specific result … which is one of the fundamental principles in practicing Reiki.

Years ago, when I was traveling in Peru, my traveling companion and I were attempting to find a bus that would take us to the ancient ruins of Pisac, outside of Cusco. It was raining pretty hard, and try as we might, we could not find the bus. We went around blocks, looking for it, asking people, but not finding the exact location of where it departed from. The rain was soaking us to our skin. We decided to turn back into Cusco for the evening and try again the next day. I told my companion that I felt this to be a definite sign—we needed to let go of this attachment to getting to our original destination and see what would occur the following day.

The next day, we found the bus to Pisac rather easily, and as we got into town, another English-speaking couple approached us and asked if we were going to the ruins. We decided to pool resources and go to the ruins together. As our guide explained to us the various sites, the woman from the couple was talking with me about her own career path. I began to tell her various paths she could take, getting very excited at being back into the realm of career counselor, part of my essential truth. The day itself seemed perfect, flowing effortlessly. The ruins were beautiful, and the woman I spoke with had achieved a degree of clarity about her path. That night and the following morning I had an incredible feeling of being in the right place at the right time. Letting go had allowed in this new and energizing experience.

4. Be curious.

I would also call this facet of discernment "cultivating curiosity." As a Reiki practitioner, one should always have a curious mind, not set to outcome. Because the practice of Reiki is greater than you and not of you, so the result of any given situation or setting is really beyond you.

When you cultivate a curious mind, you also loosen up the ego. I've heard "ego" stands for "edging God out." So when we are full of ego, not curious, not paying attention, determined to have our way, we lose out on coincidences and connections. Another way to say this is that we let go of the pre-arranged plan and yield to other possibilities, using our discernment.. We can still have a focus and a goal for what we want to achieve, but we aren't hard and fast attached to what the route has to look like to get there.

I've seen many clients change their perception of their own diagnostic condition by cultivating a more curious approach. Instead of relying solely on one way to treat their condition, they take a more integrated approach.

Sarah came to me as an eighteen-year-old recently diagnosed with bipolar disorder of the mania type. But if she hadn't been curious about the effects of the mania, she would not have come to my office. During the manic periods, she had been creating prolific works of art, exploring music, and devouring poetry. She also went from her typical introverted self into a very extroverted mode.

Sarah felt that the mania was an aspect of her, beyond the diagnosis that was creative energy that wanted expression. But she had also reached a place where she was not able to function because she could not find within her center a place to calm down and make decisions or complete tasks.

She currently is taking Lithium to manage the extreme symptoms but is working with her psychiatrist to begin also to integrate Reiki as a method to teach her how to come back to her center and to explore safely and with much curiosity that creative element that is regaining shape and form.

Being curious is also being playful, and the more play practitioners can bring into practice, while of course, maintaining a professional presence, the more potential energy is available to both them and their clients and students. I talk more on this in Tool #4, Cultivating the Creative Career.

5. Stick to one path until you have achieved some level of mastery.

From my own experience, I can say that sticking to one path, instead of going down many different ones, has allowed a depth of knowledge and wisdom to emerge. I discovered for myself that a repetitive practice on the spiritual path builds a solid foundation. Whether yoga, meditation, martial arts, journaling, etc., the continuity serves as an anchor and facilitates the discernment because you become rooted in the integrity of the practice. When new paths appear, you have a base to which to return to for contemplation and clarity.

One cultivates discernment through the practice of Reiki. You come to realize in Level 1 that your presence alone is a gift and that you have the ability to channel Universal Energy, regardless of your past experience, background, or belief system. You can travel the world from your armchair by sending Reiki in Level 2. You can begin to see the great light of Reiki in yourself in Level 3 and how it serves as a reflecting mirror for others in your life. You begin walking the master path and realize that there is no ending point to it: you are now more responsible for your words and actions and in training others.

Discernment is an ongoing process, and it is a mechanism that allows us to look at the outside world for guidance while going inward for confirmation. The more we are aware of who we are as human beings and Reiki practitioners, the more successful we are in our practice in reaching out to the world.

Exercise

A. Who are you?

The more you know what you are about, the easier discernment becomes.

You can discover more about yourself by recording yourself saying "Who are you?" (or have a friend willing to ask it to you) repeatedly in twenty- to thirty-second intervals over a five- to ten-minute period. Do thirty minutes if you really want to get to the juice! We use this technique in advanced Reiki training to get to the heart of who exactly we are beyond our roles, titles, functions.

If you can have a friend ask you the question, you can then return the favor after your session is over. It's a very profound experience for both.

Spend time journaling and reflecting after this exercise. Give yourself plenty of time for meditation, reflection, and Reiki healing.

Tool #2:
Making Space and Time for the Journey

The idea of making space and time for our journey along the healing Reiki path sounds so simple and obvious yet has quite profound ramifications. It allows for all the other aspects of discernment to become more integrated with our being. In so doing, it permits us to have more opportunities to experience different applications for utilizing Reiki.

1. Defining Space

Let's talk about space first. How do we create spaces for healing in our lives? With whom do we create them? Why do we do it and in what manner? And of course, and maybe more important, why do we fail to make the space? My whole Reiki journey has been about making that space, but what is it exactly?

Space encompasses many dimensions and forms. It can define a physical location, such as a room, a park, or a favorite café. It can cover time and the priority in our day-to-day schedule. It can hold a place in our minds in the form of a memory, for example, a delightful experience when we felt supported and loved. Space can also refer to the parts within ourselves—our hearts, our guts, our minds—where we process the emotions, memories, and experiences that flood our existence. "Making space" is a pro-active term.

It says that we will make an effort; we commit to our own healing, whether physical, mental, or spiritual, for ourselves, for our family, for our community.

When I take that leap and begin to make that space, I create room for the emotions and the feelings, like anger, grief, and despair, I may have been avoiding. Once I acknowledge my inner state, tremendous healing can and does occur.

2. Honor the Pause

It is not always easy to make space for healing.

The system of hands-on Reiki offers a tool to assist going within and staying within for a length of time. During this process of "honoring the pause," renewal and revitalization occur. Healing happens.

Taking one's time on the path is also quite important. There are many Reiki systems that have developed that combine all levels of training in one book or one weekend.

In the traditional Reiki training I was schooled in, we are taught to wait a minimum of three months between Levels 1 and 2 and at least six months between Levels 2 and 3. Level 3 is the entrance point to becoming a Reiki master apprentice, and if a student chooses that path, he or she has at least another year of shadowing the teaching, co-facilitating classes, and taking time to internalize the lessons learned in Reiki so that he or she can effectively teach it to others.

All my Level 1 students know there is a waiting period before taking the next class. It allows time for the integration of the attunements given in the first level and gives plenty of opportunities for individuals to practice on themselves, on others, and in their own space. Reiki is learning by doing, and one cannot gain complete knowledge and understanding in just one workshop—and should not hold such expectations. In between levels, I encourage students to attend practice Reiki circles/shares or participate in our monthly clinic and do as many session trades as possible.

Reading about Reiki (there are now over three thousand titles on Amazon.com alone) is helpful, but learning happens in the doing. Through the waiting and practicing, the wisdom emerges.

3. Case Story: From Session to Level 1

Troy was a fifty-one-year-old married man who had worked as a petroleum engineer in many parts of the world over the previous seven years. He had recently returned from a position in China, bringing back extra weight and unhealthy habits of smoking and drinking from the business circles there. He and his wife were beginning to start their new life in Seattle.

He came to me because he wanted to work on redefining who he was and what he could do with his life. Working as an engineer had been monetarily profitable but emotionally and physically draining. Troy had been a practitioner of meditation and yoga off and on over the years and also enjoyed swimming to help clear his mind and exercise his body. While receiving Reiki during his treatment session, he often likened it to the mental state he would experience doing the various activities mentioned. Yet, by him getting in touch with his breathing and his feeling in his body, he expressed he was able to go to a deeper level than before.

In between our sessions, Troy explored some supportive career transition books, but it wasn't until our last meeting when he realized that he might have to confront his own fear about becoming what he had started out to be ten years ago—a registered nurse, for which he had gone to school and had received a degree. But for whatever fears that arose at that time, he had also obtained a degree in engineering and had taken that path instead. He clearly stated his intention to explore the possibility of entering into healing work, and he followed through by attending a Reiki Level 1 workshop I taught to assist further his confidence and competence in walking in the shoes of that inner healer.

4. Case Story: From Level 1 to 2

Several years ago, I worked with two students, both of whom were at different stages of their Reiki journey, and the differences reinforced for me the importance of taking one's time between each level in the Reiki system.

The first student I worked with, I'll call Lisa, I met through my acting world several years ago. She had taken Level 1 from another teacher, but several years ago, she came to me to be "re-attuned" in a more traditional approach.

She's an amazing actor and an incredible human being. Her daughter, some twenty years old, has had severe learning and physical disabilities since birth, so Lisa has spent her motherhood nursing and caring and getting very acquainted with the skills needed to communicate non-verbally and psychically with her daughter. In addition, Lisa is very tapped in to the shamanic realm of existence and has deep ties to the land in Arizona.

After Reiki 1, she told me that her ability to communicate with Spirit had vastly improved and her own acting career had seen some advantages of having a technique to help center herself during and after performance.

But this day, she came in for a session to realign to Reiki, it having been at least a year since that Level 1 training. She would be ready to take on Level 2 in the coming weeks and take her daughter to the next level as well.

She had elements of her life she was finally ready to look at: an incomplete high school education, unfinished studies in painting and music, and other projects left unaccomplished. Through Insight Reiki, which we'll discuss in the next chapter, we addressed the energies around incompleteness and what that felt like to her and the liberation of being able to transcend perceived limitations and embrace the timelessness of being in Level 2 consciousness. I felt honored to witness her journey at this point and to receive a reminder that when the student is ready ... the lesson (and teacher) appears.

5. Case Story: From Level 2 to 3

The other student, Georgia, was a Reiki student I had been working with over the course of the year. She had completed her Level 2 training several months ago and was now preparing to enter into level 3 also in only a few weeks.

Just like Lisa, she wanted to prep herself energetically for the path and, while on the table, went into a deep level of shamanic consciousness, having to do with her own fears of being attacked by psychic sources. She had been in a recent car accident and was feeling that some black energy had attached itself to her in the form of an etheric bug, which would often bite away at her auric field and make her feel very vulnerable, exposed, and subject to more accidents.

It was interesting that she was perceiving in herself a limitation, that her sense of Self stopped at her auric field. Yet it was just a different understanding of limits from that expressed by Lisa, my other advanced Reiki student.

While on the table, Georgia felt her aura stretching out into the cosmos so that, if there were etheric bugs, they could have a piece of that infinite without depleting her store because of its endless nature. It was as if she was giving part away, making an offering for them, or her own consciousness that felt itself a victim or at the mercy of unexplained phenomena.

In the middle of this awareness, I started to cough and saw in my own mind's eye black goop, like tar, coming out of her, passing through my own channel, and being turned into white light. We talked about letting the space in her being now fill up with that white light and letting go of anything else that didn't serve her at this time. She ended the session confirming that she was now eager to embrace the Reiki master energy and incorporate this level of awareness into her conscious being.

I humbly bow to Troy, Georgia, and Lisa for being brave to take the journey within and to orient themselves to the levels of Reiki training and understanding that now awaited them. Taking time along the path has permitted all of them to focus on various elements of their own healing and, in so doing, creates more room for them to hold space for the various individuals they will meet and help in healing as they continue.

Exercise

A. What if?

Change follows us all wherever we go, so the idea of security is really a kind of illusion because every second of every day things are changing. Sometimes we can barely perceive them. We go day in and day out, following our routines with our family, friends, pets; nothing seems different. But cells in our bodies are dying and new ones are being created, new oxygen molecules are being exchanged, and in the greater world, something else has gone on.

So, what would it be like if by some unfortunate act of the Universe, your doctor called you up and said, "I'm really sorry, but your lab results were switched, and now that we have the correct ones in, it seems that you only have six months to live."

Yikes! What happens when you go within and just reflect on that statement? What would you do? What would you see yourself doing with only that amount of time left on the planet? What would you change? What would you keep the same?

Take some time and feel free to write down any insights that come from imagining that experience.

Then, going back within, imagine the doctor again, coming back to you and saying, "Actually, it seems you have another two to five years with your diagnosis. Sorry for the scare of only six months, but it seems you have more time." How does this change your image of what you would do? What other steps are included now that you have a little more time to finish things? What do you see?

Tool #3: Insight Reiki: Taking Reiki to the Next Level

When I began working in counseling centers on the East Coast in the early nineties, I noticed that clients avoided addressing many parts of a session. I got the feeling that what clients didn't say or show told you the most about them. I couldn't ignore the fact that much more was going on in the session than the dialogue we were exchanging. I began to sense problems lurking behind polite smiles. Sometimes I even saw what I later learned were energy fields around them, which would fluctuate in color, depending on the client's mood.

As I pursued Reiki studies, energy techniques began to ease their way into the environment of my sessions, and the basis for Insight Reiki was born.

As a client would talk about his or her emotional reactions after getting fired or left by a spouse or some other troubling event, I would begin to send Reiki to them. I would intuitively begin to sense what parts of their energetic body were holding on out of scarcity and fear. I "asked" Reiki to continue to flow during each session, and on several occasions, I was called to place my hands gently over a client's shoulders or forehead. I would ask them if they were OK to have me practice this stress reducing method I had learned.

I found presenting the Reiki and counseling techniques this way so simple and invigorating that I began to teach some of the methods to my clients. I witnessed incredible changes in their personal lives. Clients who were previously unable to achieve any true insight or direction were now able to connect with their own passions for career and life changes they needed to make for living more fully.

I initially called my technique Bodywork Counseling, but I always knew that name was a placeholder, since it was so generic. That initial name also was a misnomer of sorts because the practitioner did not perform counseling in the same way a traditionally trained counselor would. But I couldn't think of another name for the technique and didn't force one to emerge. So for several years, Reiki practitioners who went through my program also called the technique they did in session Bodywork Counseling.

But recently, Washington State changed the professional and academic requirements for practitioners who wished to call what they do "counseling." For myself, with a master's degree and years of experience in the counseling profession, I had to study and sit for a comprehensive exam to continue to offer my services.

Although I adapted, many of my practitioner students would not have such an "easy" time providing Reiki under the new constraint. I realized it was time to change the name of Bodywork Counseling because I didn't want them to have to deal with any unnecessary conflict. Still not forcing a name, just leaving space for it to come to me, one day, while practicing the technique on myself, I realized the impressions I was receiving were like insights. And so, the name Insight Reiki was born and branded.

Insight Reiki encourages an individual to get in touch with the feelings surrounding trauma, confusion, or pain that he or she is holding within the body. Balance is initiated through Reiki, which serves as the foundation of the practice. As one gets in touch with these feelings, emotions are released, which brings additional insight and clarity to the situation/issue at hand. The method can also be used on oneself to provide additional insight on current issues or problems.

People respond to the healing power of touch. It reaffirms to them the experiences of their whole being instead of just their intellect and cognition through verbal counseling alone. The physical body holds memories, fears, hopes, and dreams. Through Insight Reiki, the bio-energetic field around the client is unblocked and released and allows the client to feel or intuit what is and what is not real. The client is able to go into a 'void' or 'trance state' and find answers to many of his or her questions.

Over the last thirty years, other professional organizations, such as the European Association of Body Psychotherapy and the United States Association of Body Psychotherapy have provided support for the integration of bodywork and counseling approaches.

There are no specific limitations or ethical restrictions of utilizing counseling approaches within the confines of a Reiki session in either the code of ethics for the Associated Bodywork & Massage Professionals or the International Association of Reiki Professionals. However, I feel it should be made clear to clients that the Reiki practitioner is NOT a therapist and that Insight Reiki is NOT a substitute for therapy.

I've found that students having a background in which they've offered help to others—volunteering, professionally doing social work, nursing, or at least an equivalent amount of their own self-help work—assists the process of learning Insight Reiki because they've already encountered the necessity of having *bodicitta*, or loving kindness, when working to help someone. If they've never had this opportunity, then before they go out and see clients, I recommend at least a year or more of working with people in this capacity, giving Reiki at Reiki circles, volunteering through hospice or nursing homes, and/or doing their own therapy.

Because practitioners come to the session with Reiki as their base, they already understand what it means to have faith in a Universal Energy. That is love and light, and it guides the session so much more than the practitioner.

If you approach each session with a full and open heart, sur-rendering over to Reiki as your guide, and follow the basic protocol for opening and closing a session, then what happens in between is divine. It is an honor for you to bear witness to it.

Insight Reiki Benefits

1. Engages the healing power of touch. This therapy alone is reaffirming.

2. Is a multi-dimensional approach and can be used with diverse populations.

3. Aids in unblocking and releasing the bio-energetic field.

4. Allows the client to experience his or her whole being instead of just the intellect/cognition.

5. Reaffirms client's presence, allowing him or her to feel/intuit what is and isn't real.

6. Presents the truth for the client to deal with. A person can argue with words and avoid facing reality. But the body doesn't lie—it holds memories, fears, hopes, and dreams.

7. Facilitates the client going into the "void," often called a "trance state" and is similar to the collective unconscious Jung spoke of. Here the person will find answers to many important and pressing questions.

Like most endeavors related to bodywork, the process is difficult to intellectualize because it involves both body and mind.

Reiki practitioners certified through the Reiki Training Program become adept in using Insight Reiki in treatment sessions if a client requests it.

Case Study: Using Insight Reiki in Reiki Practice

I used Insight Reiki with my client, Paul, who was feeling a lot of anger towards being laid off, the unfairness of the seemingly unrelated circumstances affecting his life, and the out-of-control aspect to them. I asked him how the anger felt in his body, and he said like a thick dense cloud. I asked if the cloud had a sound. He made a low grumble. I had my drum and began to gently play a drumbeat behind him and encouraged him to let out that groan a little bit more. A louder groan was heard. I played the drum louder. His groans began to turn into growls. I encouraged him to continue with his growling. He began to yell now, and over the sound of his yells, anger came out as definite releases.

After several minutes, I slowed down the drumbeat and asked Paul to take a few minutes to breathe into his body and check in with what had occurred. He had released some tears along with his yells, too, and giving him some tissues and some water helped him come back into his center. A few moments later, he told me he was ready to lie on the table and allow me to place my hands on his back and head so he could go into the "real" issue of his breathing difficulties that had plagued him all his life. I encouraged him to take this process slowly. He did and went "into" his nasal passages and felt that some of the blockages there, even while he as on his side, which often caused him to feel the breathing problems even more, were dissipating. I put my hand over the middle of his upper back, or the back of the heart chakra. He said he felt as if he was coming into a place of nurturing and acceptance, and at that point, I encouraged him to become quiet in that place while the soft music in the background played on.

I remained present within him in that place for several more minutes before we concluded, did a brief check-in, and ended the session. Paul later told me that he slept very well that evening and was able to go on a retreat where he was required to sleep in bunk beds and was able actually to sleep through the night. In the past, sleeping in this arrangement would bring on an element of claustrophobia for him and cause him great difficulty in breathing and sleeping.

With Insight Reiki, a presenting symptom often obscures other, deeper issues. In this case, Paul's difficulty in breathing masked his anger about the lay-off and his anger related to other areas of his life. It also indicated his difficulty in breathing in life for himself. The session was profoundly moving, and I felt honored to be in the presence of such an awakening.

How to Do Insight Reiki for Yourself

As mentioned with the tool of discernment, a curious mind—one that is quite open and receptive to the body-mind wisdom that resides within—will aid you in doing Reiki. And be prepared to be surprised.

You'll see as you go through the following meditations (recorded to the music of Dean Evenson that is available for purchase through my Web site) the reasons polarities work so well in Insight Reiki is because, by acknowledging the conflict, we give room for it. We aren't marginalizing it or pushing it to the side. We give it space. As we "play" with both sides of the conflict, we are also giving more room for perspective … and in that making of space, Reiki can support the process of transformation.

Once you get the basics down of the body scan and observing, you can do this technique anywhere to assist in opening and releasing tension as well as providing insight to problems that arise in your life.

Taking the Insight Reiki journey is like learning to scuba dive. You will encounter new things on your first dive, and subsequent explorations will go even deeper and open you up to greater parts of your awareness.

But just as with diving, you need to begin with a good guide. So let me assist you on these first discoveries.

You might want to have a journal nearby to record your initial impressions. Later, the experience of going within will happen much more readily, so don't be too hard on yourself in the beginning. Treat each meditation like an exercise.

1. Exercise: Basic body scan

Take your time. Connect with your breath. Get comfortable, either sitting in a relaxed position or lying down. Inhale deeply. As you come into your center, begin the process at your own pace of scanning down and through your entire being. You will start at the top of your head and finish at the tips of your toes, all the while noticing what is at each part of your body.

From the top of your crown, gently begin observing as you scan down your head, your face, the back of your neck, down through your shoulders, your back, across your chest, down through your abdomen, your hips, down through your lower back, thighs, knees, ankles, and feet.

Begin to become aware of whatever part of you calls out to you at the moment. It could be an area of tension. It could be a particular symptom you were experiencing. Perhaps it's a flash of heat or a color. Simply note what calls out to you.

Now, spend a few moments honing in, going closer to this part of you that wants acknowledgement. Begin to breathe into this space. Where the breath flows, the Reiki goes. Let the area expand in size as you go in deeper, bringing your curious mind with you, just noticing.

As you go in closer, just be in the sensation for several moments. Notice if it begins to change or give you particular insight on the problem or symptom at hand. Maybe words come to you, maybe images. Simply become aware. And then thank that part of you for sharing.

Continue on with the next part of your body, paying attention and going deeper whenever a part calls you.

Once you have finished, down at your toes, back out and away. Begin to inhabit what I call the "neutral space." Let your mind daydream for a while.

That was good work in observing. Now, take a break for a few moments, listen to the music, and settle into your breath. Good.

Now, perform the scan again from head to toe. Notice what has changed, what is different.

Bring your breath back into center and take your time coming out of this exploration. Feel free to journal anything that came up for you.

2. Exercise: Polarities

This second exercise repeats the body scan and brings over polarities to see what other information your body/mind might have for you.

As before, take your time. Connect with your breath. Get comfortable, either sitting in a relaxed position or lying down. Inhale deeply. As you come into your center, begin the process at your own pace of scanning down and through your entire being. You will start at the top of your head and finish at the tips of your toes, all the while noticing what is at each part of your body.

From the top of your crown, gently begin observing as you scan down your head, your face, the back of your neck, down through your shoulders, your back, across your chest, down through your abdomen, your hips, down through your lower back, thighs, knees, ankles, and feet.

Begin to become aware of whatever part of you calls out to you at the moment. It could be an area of tension. It could be a particular symptom you were experiencing. Perhaps it's a flash of heat or a color. Simply note what calls out to you.

Now, spend a few moments honing in, going closer to this part of you that wants acknowledgement. Begin to breathe into this space. Where the breath flows, the Reiki goes. Let the area expand in size as you go in deeper, bringing your curious mind with you, just noticing.

As you go in closer, just be in the sensation for several moments. Notice if it begins to change or give you a particular insight on the problem or symptom at hand.

Now, notice another part of your body, perhaps if you are focusing on the top of your body, notice what the bottom part is doing. Or if you are in the front, what is happening in the back? Or if you are on one side, what is happening on the opposite?

Bring your breath and attention into this opposite part of you and give it room to expand.

Breathe deeply and gently, bringing that curious mind. Notice what happens as you let it expand into the original part you started with.

Bring a child-like wonder to the experience and begin to play back and forth with both parts, superimposing each on the other.

Notice if it begins to change or give you particular insight on the problem or symptom at hand. Maybe words come to you, maybe images. Simply become aware. And then thank that part of you for sharing.

Now, backing out and away, inhabit the "neutral space." Let your mind daydream.

That was good work in observing, exploring, seeing what begins to take place. Now, take a break for a few moments, listen to the music, and settle into your breath. Good.

Now, perform the scan again from head to toe. Notice what has changed, what is different.

Bring your breath back into center and take your time coming out of this exploration. Feel free to journal anything that came up for you.

3. Exercise: Heart and solar plexus chakras

This third exercise repeats the body scan and explores what additional insight your heart and solar plexus chakras might have to give.

Take your time. Connect with your breath. Get comfortable, either sitting in a relaxed position or lying down. Inhale deeply. As you come into your center, begin the process at your own pace of scanning down and through your entire being. You will start at the top of your head and finish at the tips of your toes, all the while noticing what is at each part of your body.

From the top of your crown, gently begin observing as you scan down your head, your face, the back of your neck, down through your shoulders, your back, across your chest, down through your abdomen, your hips, down through your lower back, thighs, knees, ankles, and feet.

Begin to become aware of whatever part of you calls out to you at the moment. It could be an area of tension. It could be a particular symptom you were experiencing. Perhaps it's a flash of heat or a color. Simply note what calls out to you.

Now, spend a few moments honing in, going closer to this part of you that wants acknowledgement. Begin to breathe into this space. Where the breath flows, the Reiki goes. Let the area expand in size as you go in deeper, bringing your curious mind with you, just noticing.

As you go in closer, just be in the sensation for several moments. Notice if it begins to change or give you a particular insight on the problem or symptom at hand.

If you have a particular area of your life you want more insight on, bring that up now as well. Bring the thought or image into the center of your heart chakra. Breathe into the heart, take a hand, and apply Reiki into the area. Bring your breath and attention into the heart and give it room to expand. Breathe deeply and gently, bringing that curious mind.

Notice what begins to occur. Maybe words come to you, maybe images. Simply become aware. Then thank the heart for sharing.

Now, bring the thought or image into the center of your solar plexus chakra. Breathe into the solar plexus, the center of your being, the abdomen, and take a hand and apply Reiki into the area. Bring your breath and attention into this area and give it room to expand. Breathe deeply and gently, bringing that curious mind.

Notice what begins to occur. Maybe words come to you, maybe images. Simply become aware. Then thank the solar plexus for sharing.

Now, backing out and away, inhabit the "neutral space." Let your mind daydream.

That was good work in observing, exploring, seeing what begins to take place.

Now, take a break for a few moments, listen to the music, and settle into your breath. Good.

Now, perform the scan again from head to toe. Notice what has changed, what is different.

Bring your breath back into center and take your time coming out of this exploration. Feel free to journal anything that came up for you.

4. Exercise: Higher self or child/elder self

This fourth exercise repeats the body scan and incorporates the wisdom of your higher self or that of your child/elder self.

Take your time. Connect with your breath. Get comfortable, either sitting in a relaxed position or lying down. Inhale deeply. As you come into your center, begin the process at your own pace of scanning down and through your entire being. You will start at the top of your head and finish at the tips of your toes, all the while noticing what is at each part of your body.

From the top of your crown, gently begin observing as you scan down your head, your face, the back of your neck, down through your shoulders, your back, across your chest, down through your abdomen, your hips, down through your lower back, thighs, knees, ankles, and feet.

Begin to become aware of whatever part of you calls out to you at the moment. It could be an area of tension. It could be a particular symptom you were experiencing. Perhaps it's a flash of heat or a color. Simply note what calls out to you.

Now, spend a few moments honing in, going closer to this part of you that wants acknowledgement. Begin to breathe into this space. Where the breath flows, the Reiki goes. Let the area expand in size as you go in deeper, bringing your curious mind with you, just noticing.

As you go in closer, just be in the sensation for several moments. Notice if it begins to change or give you a particular insight on the problem or symptom at hand.

If you have a particular area of your life you want more insight on, bring that up now as well.

Invite the presence of the wisdom of your higher self, your guide, into your being. You might explore first with the insight a wise teacher might give you, maybe your elder self. I'll often use my ninety-year-old self and ask what she would say.

Breathe deeply and gently, bringing that curious mind.

Notice what begins to occur. Maybe words come to you, maybe images. Simply become aware. Then thank your wise self for sharing.

Now, invite the wisdom of your child-like self, your nine-year-old. What would he or she say?

Breathe deeply and gently, bringing that curious mind. Notice what begins to occur. Maybe words come to you, maybe images. Simply become aware. Then thank your wise self for sharing.

Now, backing out and away, inhabit the "neutral space." Let your mind daydream.

That was good work in observing, exploring, seeing what begins to take place.

Now, take a break for a few moments, listen to the music, and settle into your breath. Good.

Now, perform the scan again from head to toe. Notice what has changed, what is different.

Bring your breath back into center and take your time coming out of this exploration. Feel free to journal anything that came up for you.

5. Exercise: Shamanic shape-shifting

This last exercise, a form of shamanic shape-shifting, helps you change your viewpoint, thus clearing the way to resolve conflicts, gain insight into another person's perspective, or as often used in shamanic circles, gather information to better understand a situation.

Begin with connecting with the breath, taking your time to center, giving yourself Reiki to relax. You can perform the Basic Body Scan listed above.

When you get to the place where you feel light and relaxed, ask the higher self of the person whose perspective you wish to understand for permission.

Wait a few moments. Then as effortlessly as the breath, shift your perspective and awareness into the eyes of the other person.

Breathe deeply, as if inhabiting the other's skin for a few moments.

Now, see yourself staring back at yourself.

See how the other sees you, what he or she thinks looking at you. Notice what you-as-the-other notices, objectively. Notice how you feel in your body, in your mind from this vantage point.

Become aware of what the other person might say to you or what he or she has said to you and your reactions to those statements. Just take it in as a witness, an observer.

Continue to breathe and to acknowledge all that comes. Spend a few more moments here in the breath, from this perspective. Breathe deeply and gently, bringing that curious mind.

Notice what begins to occur. Maybe words come to you, maybe images. Simply become aware.

Now, thank your person for allowing you to take this point of view and for sharing. Release the other, and as you do, bring your breath and awareness back into the fullness of yourself.

Now, backing out and away, inhabit the "neutral space." Let your mind daydream.

That was good work in observing, exploring, seeing what begins to take place.

Now take a break for a few moments, listen to the music, and settle into your breath. Good.

Now, perform the scan again from head to toe. Notice what has changed, what is different.

Bring your breath back into center and take your time coming out of this exploration. Feel free to journal anything that came up for you.

You've now taken several journeys into exploring the greater realm of your being. I hope you have received the insight you have needed. Know that you can repeat this whole journey at any time you need, to or you can simply work with each exercise separately.

Using Insight Reiki on yourself and others will increase the element of loving kindness within your being, making you a greater conduit for reaching out to the world as you continue to do your healing work.

Tool #4: Cultivating the Creative Career

Whether you make Reiki your full- or part-time vocation, you are creating a career that is distinctly different from the forty-hour work week of a traditional employer. If you go full-time, you will be self-employed because no structures exist (yet) where you can get a paying job as a Reiki master or practitioner. If you work part-time in doing Reiki, you may have a "normal" job in another area, but you still will be involved in some level of self-employment.

By pursuing a creative career in Reiki, you will do work that invigorates you, recharges you, and makes you want to get up in the morning and "go to work." You will make the world a better place because you do work you love. I feel, in the practice of Reiki, that there is no right or wrong way to create that career, as long as it sustains you and allows you to do this work in the world.

Life is a short, wonderful existence—or can be. Unfortunately, as a career counselor, I've met many people who are unhappy in their occupations. Their struggle impacts their family and friends, and by default, the communities around them.

Think of the worker who is stressed out during the day, influencing his co-workers around him. Then, after work, he goes into a supermarket to buy groceries and, because he is still stressed from the job, takes out his angst on the staff in the store and people around him. As he grumbles in his car on the way home, perhaps he is making bad driving choices. The stress of that job has now affected many dozens of people, who, in effect, may have passed on that angst to dozens more.

Reiki as a full- or part-time vocation can offer the world a bit of sanctuary for both the practitioner and recipient, rippling out waves of peace to many others in proximity.

But before you make that jump into Reiki employment and go and get that business license, some level of self-assessment is in order. All the students who complete the Reiki Training Program must attend a business class to create their own plan of action.

The first place we start in defining your creative career is to assess where you are at in your own career process.

Cycles of the Seasons as a Guide to Your Creative Career Process

A helpful model is to use the four seasons to see where you fit in. This organic cycle occurs both inside and outside of us and is not separate or apart from our concerns. I have found that, although it might be spring or summer in the environment, people contemplating a career change or modification tend to be in either the fall or winter stage of their own change cycle.

1. In the **Fall** stage, they often feel scared, angry, victimized, and cynical about their career future. Fall is a place of being in the doldrums. They may be unwilling or unable to change from a job or career identity and move ahead. Eventually, just as the trees shed their leaves, a person in fall will have to let go—of a job (whether in getting laid off, being fired, or independently choosing to leave) and all that entails. When someone is in fall, he or she often hits bottom with depression, which people in this period often fear. Having sadness and

mourning what they are leaving is completely natural, although understandably uncomfortable. Fall is a time when individuals often need to create an exit plan, and some may find attending support groups or therapy aid their process.

As in nature, fall naturally gives way to winter.

2. **Winter** behavior is often characterized by introversion, depression, and being in limbo. Some have called this a "cocooning" stage. Nothing seems to be going on externally, but much work is occurring internally. Winter encourages you to spend time alone in reflection and begin to take a look at what you have done and what you haven't done. Winters can last a long time, and consider that, in nature, there are areas of the world where winters are the dominant landscape.

I have found that when some people skip seasons and do not allow themselves a winter in which to reflect or cultivate the resources and contacts they need for moving into the spring phase, they find themselves dissatisfied with a new job that doesn't seem to fit and wonder what went wrong.

Some people find they are in the season of winter for the good part of a year or more, which makes taking action difficult. They may find it becomes easier to put off making the decisions necessary for their goal than it is to act on those decisions. Some days they have hardly enough energy to do anything, let alone consider a new life path. The important thing to remember during this time is that the potential is there. What I encourage my clients to do while they are in this stage is to tap into the other aspects of what winter has to offer: quiet excitement, the possibility of a new beginning, listening to their inner voice, and the courage just to be. This may be a time in which you pursue contemplative work, like art or writing, meditating, Insight Reiki, or praying. Being in one's winter is *not* the time to go for the dream job. It is a time to utilize the resources at your disposal, whether they be healthcare benefits, support groups, or a part-time transition job. Reading inspirational books, such as *Callings* by Greg Levoy or *Creating the Work You Love* by Rick Jarow, may help, and going for additional individual counseling can provide insight into your process.

Eventually, even the most frozen wasteland receives a bit of sun, and the first glimpses of spring will appear. They may be brief and passing moments for people who still remain in winter, but they will come. When they do, I advise people to tap into that renewal of energy and begin to explore their options.

3. I refer to **Spring** as the "getting ready" phase. People entering spring might create a résumé of their past work to help them see their marketable skills and experiences. They may need to begin taking classes to update outmoded skills. Conducting informational interviews with individuals in fields that are interesting to them will help bring greater clarity to their career goals. Finally, I feel an important part of the spring energy is to work with the creative force, whether it is painting, dancing, singing, or writing to act as kindling for the fire that can take them into the next stage of summer.

4. When you are in a **Summer** part of your life or career, you are active, extroverted, growing, "going for it," and filled with energy. Our culture views this stage as the norm of behavior and the other three seasons as aberrations. But like the climate in the Northwest, where I live, summer often comes in fits and starts and may last only a short while.

The important thing to remember is that in *all* phases of the career/life cycle, growth is occurring. Fall and winter are internal periods of growth, spring and summer are eternal manifestations. With that realization, my hope is that individuals going through career transition will realize that there is no good or bad to their experience.

Each phase in the seasonal cycle has certain lessons to teach us. When we acknowledge these lessons instead of hurrying through them, we are honoring the natural process that is occurring within ourselves. We are cultivating the creative career, which is the process that is occurring as we recognize the missing pieces of our lives and begin to put them together to create our own unique life puzzle.

Using the Artist's Way to Challenge Limiting Beliefs

When I was in my late fall/winter phase in the last months of working full-time for an employer, wondering how I was ever going to make my dream of a Reiki training program come alive, I had a hard time trusting fully in my ability to maintain the creative energy necessary for building such a vision.

On a hunch, I enrolled in a ten-week series using Julia Cameron's book, *The Artist's Way*, as the foundation. A Reiki master colleague of mine facilitated it, so I felt there would be plenty to relate to even if the concept of considering myself as an artist was strange and foreign at the time.

Cameron's book is based on the model of the twelve-step program. Week by week, you go through various exercises designed to challenge your beliefs and limitations around your creative potential. The Reiki master who facilitated had all of us perform Reiki on ourselves and each other before we started class in a meditation. The sharing of our fears, hopes, and dreams was facilitated by this energy work, and the rest of each class consisted of some creative activity—dancing, chanting, sculpting, drawing, or making collages. Then, in between classes, we were required to do the "journeywork" necessary: We kept "Morning Pages," journals in which we wrote each morning to capture more of our process of self-discovery. To fill back our wells, we were required to take ourselves on our own "Artist Date," a time we would set aside to explore by ourselves a place that would feed our creative souls. I initially went to places like art supply and fabric stores, then gradually became more adventurous and attended art shows, sculpture parks, and out-of-the-way museums.

The practice of setting aside time to write and time to indulge in creative pursuit began to create space in my life for that inner artist to emerge. As I wrote down my inner thoughts each morning, I was creating a record of what needed to change in my life to bring more of that artist to the forefront. Daily Reiki practice and meeting with our Reiki Artist's Way class provided the supportive energy to allow our true selves to have space to emerge.

In the middle of the series, I knew I wanted to offer this class to the students and clients I worked with. That desire, along with my own creative urges, fueled me through the remainder of the series, and towards the end of the class, any insecurities I had about my artistic merit had vanished.

I enrolled from there in a women's retreat to create medicine shields out on the magnificent Pacific Ocean at a sleepy hamlet called La Push. I reclaimed my inner artist, called "Crystal Sky." It was there I created what is called a medicine shield out of various objects I had brought as well as found objects on the beach. This is the poem that spoke to me as I created it:

Becoming Crystal Sky

My shield is my guardian and protector.

She presents me with all that is beautiful and strong about myself.

Lovingly was she created, guided by the invisible hands of those that have weaved many eons before.

Beads represent that tears can be beautiful.

The animals are the guardians as we go into battle.

The blue is the sky; it is the potential of a storm to voice itself.

The feathers take away the bad energy received and retain that which is good and helpful.

The face is the face of man, of god, of us all, so that when attacked, the aggressor will remember his or her humanity and back off.

I am Crystal Sky.

I am a warrior.

And I am a healer of this planet.

I am an artist and I am a lover,

Helping humanity in its evolution

Of consciousness and understanding.

My mother is the Earth and

My father is the sky and

Together they made me light in matter

To shine as a beacon for all that's true and beautiful

And perfect of humans at this time.

From that experience, I was on fire with enthusiasm and enrolled in a weeklong study of painting with acrylics where I created over twenty pieces of art.

As I emerged from spring into summer, there was no turning back from the creative source. It helped to build structure around the Reiki Training Program and infused my world as a teacher, spilling over into each class I would teach.

I do feel creative and spiritual energy come from the same source. How one channels and incorporates that energy make us the unique individuals we are. Sometimes, it is necessary to question outmoded beliefs and patterns of living in order to help open the channel for that force, just as Reiki does, in clearing the path for an individual's higher truth.

Here are some things to remember in facilitating and partici-pating in the creative journey:

Being Authentic

Show up,

Drop the mask,

Shine the truth,

Ever last.

Remember your heart

From within the shine

Growing Radiance

Birthright Divine.

Speaking your truth

In word or phrase

Serves to inspire

For all your days.

Standing so tall

Serves others to be

Fully as humans

Just like you and me.

The channel you are,

The channel you flow,

The channel you heal,

The channel you know

Rest upon the ground.

Giving time to pause

Restores body-mind,

Reduces any flaws,

Removes your resistance

To feeling your power.

Open to silence

This very hour

When life throws delusions

And you can't see clear.

Come back to the breath,

Bringing love very near.

Let go of trying.

Effort is gone.

Release is the answer.

Exercise: Releasing the Effort

One of the first steps in working with Reiki involves what I call "ego management." "Ego" standing for "Edging God Out" … whatever God means to you. The more you are in your ego, the more you are edging God out, the less you are in Reiki flow. Hence, the need for you to get out of your own way. That's probably the single biggest challenge of practicing Reiki. First-year novices or those with ten years experience, we all have egos if we exist in modern society and aren't hibernating in a secluded cave. So we all must constantly manage our egos.

1. With this exercise, begin to think of something you've tried really hard to achieve in your life—an education, a promotion, a relationship, a breakthrough, etc.

2. Think about all the people, processes, efforts, time, money, etc. spent towards this goal.

3. Feel that with your entire being. Notice how occupied your body and mind feel, perhaps how tired, or maybe energized. Whatever the feeling, just notice it, head to toe, while also being curious if any other parts of your body also feel full from this external exertion.

4. Now, offer up all that effort. See it wrapped into a ball, perhaps surrounded by some bands keeping your great effort in one place, and give it to the Universe, to the space above you, blowing it as if you would blow on a blooming dandelion, releasing all of the seeds across a field.

5. Feel how it is to let go of the effort. Breathe it deeply. Let go, and on the inhale, let in the expanse of Universal Life Force, filling all of your world with light, love, and support.

6. With another inhalation, let more of that light expand. Notice how much lighter you feel, how room in your being has been made by your offering up your efforts and giving yourself permission to receive extra support and light.

7. Close your eyes and notice if any additional insights or images come to you regarding the efforts released.

8. If any do, thank your higher consciousness. If none arise, know you can return to this place at any time for further insight.

Tool #5: Attending and Establishing Reiki Circles and Shares in Your Community

During my Reiki career, I've been part of and have facilitated several hundred circles, or shares, as they are often called. People from all walks of life, all socioeconomic classes, political divisions, cultural and religious backgrounds, come together to share in the giving and receiving of healing energy. We might meet together as strangers, and then after only two hours, we've bonded through a mutual exchange and respect for a force that is much greater than each individual.

Back when I started Reiki, my teacher held her circles as more of a social outlet. The gatherings were often quite chatty with practitioners talking about the various comings and goings of their day while they laid their hands on and over each of the clients on the table. I didn't know any different, that being my first foray into Reiki.

But after months of attending her circles, we started getting clients who had quite serious issues like cancer, Turret's Syndrome, MS, etc. I mentioned to my teacher that perhaps we needed a quiet room for the circle to take place for individuals who had such diseases.

The quiet Reiki circle was where I first realized the immense possibility of group healing work. The individuals who soaked in twenty to thirty minutes of such treatments left without pain, and those who attended several circles began reporting that their pain and processes were subsiding.

I was hooked. As I began teaching students of my own, my circles were all quiet with gentle music in the background. Soon after starting my own circles, I began to see they also played a huge marketing role in building my business. Potential students and clients would come to a circle, invest two hours of their time, perhaps make a small donation, receive the amazing benefit of group healing, and then be curious and intrigued so much that they would sign up for a class or a private session.

I didn't think of the Reiki circles as marketing events because they gave me so much joy in bringing people together and facilitating my own healing as well. Yet, I realized that they are an important part of establishing oneself in the Reiki community. As informal events, they allow individuals to meet and greet and participate in healing and get a feel for who you are and what the process of Reiki is all about.

1. What Is a Reiki Circle?

For those new to Reiki, a circle, or share, is a group of Reiki practitioners simultaneously practicing Reiki on a recipient for a set amount of time, usually fifteen to twenty minutes. The recipient then exchanges places with a practitioner until all in the group have received their treatment.

Strangers bond and healing is facilitated. It literally is magic in action. I also feel it's one of the best ways to help facilitate world peace by breaking down boundaries in a safe manner and allowing individuals to help each other.

2. Setting Up a Circle

I've attended many other Reiki circles by other practitioners and masters, and everyone has a unique style. My favorites are those in which some sort of refreshment is offered, like tea and/or light snacks. The music sets the tone. Depending on the space, you might have candles or ambient lighting.

Above all, you create a safe space for the group healing exploration. Living rooms, furnished basements, community centers, and practitioners' treatment spaces have all become circles. Years back we even had a rotating Reiki circle in each other's living rooms. It's a wonderful way of bringing extra light and healing into a space. We've experimented with live music (which is simply wonderful!), healing lights, healing pets (for those attending who don't have allergies), incorporating other healing traditions like Shamanism, crystals, and aromatherapy.

Clearing the space in between sessions is an important part of keeping the energy flowing and the space a sanctuary. I have both rose water and sage that I will smudge. Rose water is usually my choice because it is not as offensive an aroma as sage and can quickly be sprayed in and around the group.

Chimes, bells and ting-shaws (Tibetan cymbals used to mark the beginning/ending of a ritual) are sound instruments that also can be used at the end of each session, to mark the closing as well as to gently cleanse the space.

It is important if you do mix modalities to let your attendees know that they can have a choice to receive or refuse. Setting healthy boundaries for the circle creates optimum healing space.

I used to facilitate a sound healing Reiki circle, called Reiki Soundscape, with live musicians and instruments available for participants to use. At one circle, a practitioner came in and started banging mercilessly on the drum, shaking all of us up. Another practitioner began to do shamanic psychic surgery with loud cries that also disrupted the flow. Both instances encouraged me to create a flyer with guidelines for practitioners in coming to an open circle. Loud, excessive noise was not a part of the circle, so it was stated in the guidelines and briefly gone over in the introduction each time.

3. How to Get the Word Out about Your Circle

When I started, the Internet was not mainstream. So I made little flyers and put them at the corner metaphysical bookstore. I sent a press release to the local paper and set a lot of healing intention that my circle would be a success.

That first circle drew over fifteen people. I was in awe. They found me through those two avenues alone. And from that first circle, the foundation for my future in teaching Reiki was laid.

Fast forward to now, where we do have all these other means of letting others know we do this work. Multitudes of Reiki networking Web sites abound, and even Craigslist allows you to post events for free.

The old paper flyer still has a place in letting others know about your circle, giving people something they can hold on to. I advise my students who are building their practices to use both methods. Experiment, explore. Ask how your attendees found out about your circle. See what works for you.

And remember to keep track of your audience. A simple mailing list is adequate for newcomers, but you will need to build a way to organize the information you receive. I personally recommend both an email and "snail mail" list so that, as your practice grows, you can send out messages of upcoming classes, circles, and other events you are offering. Some people prefer email, others a postcard. For those tech savvy, you might think about Facebook or Twitter contacts as well.

You never know what will come from inviting the general public to your circles, who you will meet, what networks you will create. From the two veterans who attended my circle years ago, our Reiki for Veterans program got its jump-start.

I also have encouraged participants to bring their friends and family as well, an impromptu Reiki education for those who are curious. They might not participate in the circle, but they can certainly receive a session and sit off to the side and watch. During breaks, they will often ask questions or simply bask in the energy that is generated.

4. Circles as Public Relations and Community Organization Training

Facilitating a Reiki circle is an excellent way for you, as a budding practitioner, to build your public relations skills as well. You must organize the event, market it, and then facilitate with grace and ease. Welcome to the world of self-promotion as a Reiki professional.

Each circle gets easier and easier, but in the beginning, you might feel overwhelmed. Shadow another facilitator for a while. Ask to co-facilitate and get a feel for the flow and for what details they have to keep track of. Take notes!

Reiki circles are grass-roots community organizing. But it's important to keep a regular and posted schedule for your circles. People appreciate consistency and will more easily remember the dates of your sessions. Your reliability provides a foundation for you to present yourself as a professional business as well as to assist in the building of community. When you pull people together from such different spheres, you are building a healing community that can have a voice to share with the world.

Every Reiki talk I have ever done, whether in a Level 1 class, bookstore, expo, or corporate office, has involved a Reiki circle of some kind, even if I use chairs instead of massage tables to demonstrate the effects of Reiki.

For some circles, having practitioners pre-register and limiting the number might be a solution to holding a circle in a small space. For others, having them drop in is more appropriate and lends itself to a more casual and formal affair.

In holding a Reiki circle, you are building a tribe, so to speak. Become creative with ways in which you can reach out to this group and keep them informed of your offerings.

In the summer, we have provided circles outdoors as well, and holding such a circle is a very magical and powerful experience. Not only are you channeling the healing vibration of Reiki, but you are also tapping into the soothing and grounding energy of the land upon which you are standing. After 9/11, several Reiki colleagues and I went to a public park and brought our Reiki table to provide free sessions. Our signs read "Inner Peace Starts from Within." Many of the passers-by in the park were very grateful to have the support of healing energy at such a time of national crisis.

5. Touching the World through Reiki Circles

In that same vein, we have also held monthly circles for global healing. Instead of having clients lie on tables, we would take world events and places and peoples that were in crisis and put them in the center of our circle where we were seated and send healing energy from a distance. The impressions of each "send" were often quite profound. I've heard it said that for every hour of news that you watch or read you should balance with sending healing. This circle was the result of that affirmation.

A group out of Seattle, Global Earthsend, apparently has over fifty thousand Reiki practitioners connected worldwide via the

Internet who send healing energy to a particular part of the world each Friday night. Again, powerful community involvement is working for world healing.

Before beginning your larger circle within the greater community, allow room for dialogue. Get to meet the other participants. What brings them to your space? Get to know the amazing people who share the same passion for healing that you do. We started the Reiki Fellowship that way, building upon many shared experiences in Reiki circles.

6. Social Significance of Circles

Circles cost considerably less to the individual than private sessions. But the depth and breadth of where a client can go in an individual treatment certainly exceeds that of a fifteen-minute Reiki circle treatment.

Yet, if you consider that most circles are donation based, and if one was to attend an event each week, the monthly cost would be ten times less than paying for private health insurance. Circles are not a substitute for traditional health care, but they certainly serve as a supplement for many.

The perception of "stranger" dies in such an environment. People come together to send healing energy to each other, to the world. Their individual differences are blurred into the healing collective. No one ego stands out. No one is greater than the other. Each person may have certain skills that differ, but together they form a healing unit that amplifies all those individual abilities and makes the unit function as a whole.

Circles are places of deep healing and self-discovery. They provide a safe environment of support and embrace and love reminiscent of being held by a universal mother. The circle becomes the receptacle for a recipient's self-discovery and healing: "How do I feel about being held by those I had perceived as strangers? These people are now coming together to help me on my path. They have never met me, and yet they hold me." Each one in turn receives from the group in an equal balance of giving and receiving. There are no expectations.

There are circles being held all over the world, in many different environments. I feel that as time goes on, we will see more of them in traditional arenas like hospitals, corporate spaces, and educational institutions because circles do offer an immediate experience of stress-reduction and relaxation.

So stay tuned. Keep doing your work. Hold a circle. Build your practice. Reiki circles as social healing phenomena are beginning to reach their potential. Continue to watch the world transform through the building of healing community and the sharing of Universal Energy.

Part II
Taking Reiki to the Mainstream

Setting a Reiki Standard

Over the years I have received several emails from Reiki masters and interested parties asking about why my healing arts vocational school, the Reiki Training Program, offered state registration for Reiki practitioners and masters.

No official certification is required in the state of Washington, or in any other state other than Florida and Utah. To practice Reiki in those states, you need either to be a Licensed Massage Practitioner or to have completed a minimum of one hundred hours of Reiki training. But my background training includes a master's in counseling and education, and I worked within vocational and community education centers for years. I have seen the importance in setting a standard for education in training, hence my efforts to get the Reiki Training Program licensed.

Each student that attends either program that we offer, Registered Reiki Practitioner and Certified Reiki Master, gets registered with the state of Washington for completing a certain number of training hours required of each curriculum. I also recently received accreditation from the Washington Association of Mental Health Counselors to offer continuing education credit to counselors who take Reiki training through my school. The requirements aren't difficult to attain—several workshops, individual and group Reiki practice, and advisory sessions to keep track of progress. There is no pass or fail. The practitioner program takes about six months, the master program about twelve months. Although that is the minimum, some of my students take a lot longer between workshops, building up lots of additional experience before they go out into the world and market themselves.

Since starting the Reiki path, I've seen a lot of changes in the field. The material being taught, for the most part, still remains the same, but changes in the ways in which it is taught have compelled me to establish a credited institution. Students can download all three levels of Reiki from their computer and become a Reiki master in one weekend. There are other poor quality Reiki training programs because often Reiki masters do not offer any follow-up practice in the form of Reiki practice circles or advisory sessions. This is imperative to a Reiki student's course of study—accountability as well as practice to help the student grow into his or her potential as a healer.

I have also seen Reiki advertised as a sensual/sexual practice. I have heard stories from some of my students of their energy-work practitioner not practicing good boundaries within the therapeutic relationship. How does the public know the difference between a sensual practice and a strictly therapeutic one if no standard defines it? The profession of massage underwent a similar analysis and self-examination process in achieving state licensure.

I have found that students who use the fast and easy methods often end up in my classes, taking them over because they have no idea what they have been attuned to or learned in such a short period of time.

As it is, I teach each level in a full day, but each student must wait months between levels, and usually a greater amount of time between the advanced levels.

The Reiki Training Program standard is a start, a work in process as I continue to learn and enhance the courses. It is a model I hope other Reiki masters will follow and use to help take Reiki into the next century.

Having a standard permits Reiki practitioners to feel competent, mastering many of the principles explained in Part I. Because of that mastery, they are then able to be greater channels of healing to bring the much needed light to this world.

Taking Reiki on the Road

One day, as I was meandering downtown through the streets of Seattle, where I live, I noticed the ubiquitous Starbucks stores on each corner and thought, why couldn't Reiki strive for the same type of presence in our society? I was reminded of the spiritual truth that if you can dream it, it can become a reality. So, I let my creative imagination go wild.

I imagined mobile Reiki healing venues where people could come in and receive a short, twenty-minute session while reclining in a comfortable chair with some sort of sleep mask and headphones to take them into a deeper sense of relaxation while a practitioner provided a Reiki treatment. The idea would be similar to the "massage bars" in airports, but instead of facing forward in a massage chair, recipients would be reclining. With the addition of eye and ear covering and a warm blanket, the recipient would be able to tune out external distractions and tune in to his or her inner healing.

To fulfill my vision, I knew I would need a team of practitioners, rather than just my solo self. I created an organization called the Reiki Fellowship and invited graduates of my Reiki Training Program as well as other practitioners from around the country to join in our mission of "Connecting the World with Reiki." The activities of the group include educational outreach and participation at local festivals and expositions. In addition, we have a Web site where members post their biographies and links to their own Web sites. Annual membership fees offset the costs of entry fees and needed equipment. Since its creation in the summer of 2007, the Reiki Fellowship has become a group of more than fifty members across the US.

The group's first outreach activity was providing Mobile Reiki sessions at several local festivals. We pooled our resources and purchased a portable ten-by-ten display booth and banners and brought folding chairs. Doing Reiki in the hustle and bustle of a fair is a very different experience than working within the quiet confines of your own private office. Each time we set up our display, we'd learn something new about working out in the open.

For a successful festival experience, it is essential to schedule practitioners to man the booth as well as practitioners to give treatments. The booth crew can field questions and talk about Reiki, give out brochures, sell items, take pictures, encourage visitors to sign mailing lists, and respond to unanticipated events like bad weather, wind knocking over the tent, and brochures blowing around.

At festivals, practitioners need to realize that they will encounter noises beyond their control. There is crowd noise, music, utility trucks backing up with beepers, and the interested people coming up to you to ask you what you are doing. As a practitioner, it's vital to remain grounded, and if noise is a bother, that you have a way to shut it out with a device such as an iPod that has serene music pre-recorded on it. The person you are giving Reiki to should also have such a device, as well as eye covering to block out light and a blanket or sheet that not only acts as insulation against the weather but also helps define treatment space.

After successfully presenting and practicing at four neighborhood festivals, we felt we had enough experience to provide sessions in shifts during a two-day health exposition at a Seattle convention center. Fifteen practitioners performed over four hundred sessions.

Only three of the recipients declined to be included on our mailing list! Since that time, each practitioner has reported several appointments and/or students resulting from this outreach. That's about a 10 percent return on the effort involved.

During the expo, practitioner Peggy Snow ran into a teenage girl she had treated earlier in the day and found the girl excitedly sharing with her friends what she had experienced in the Reiki session. The girls were anxious to have Peggy share information about Reiki, her work, and the Reiki Fellowship.

The experience of doing Mobile Reiki outdoors and in a large convention center reinforced what we know as practitioners—when you create the space for healing, Reiki flows, regardless of the noise and activities going on around you. With these experiences under our belts, several of us decided to take Mobile Reiki to the next level—into corporate America.

Reiki Master Tom Brophy was instrumental in opening the corporate door for the Reiki Fellowship and Mobile Reiki. He approached the Human Resources Department of a large Seattle corporation, explained Reiki, and suggested it would be a great benefit for workers going through the stress of potential lay-offs. HR was open to the idea as long as the company didn't have to pay for it, so the arrangement was made to have employees pay the Reiki practitioners directly for their services. Tom agreed to handle scheduling of appointments and put out the word to employees through inter-office email that Reiki sessions would be available the following week. Employees signed up for twenty-minute treatments during their break times. He found a suitable room in his building that was quiet and insulated from the noises of the surrounding office for sessions.

Reiki Master Jennifer Yost and I provided the treatments. On the first day, she and I saw four clients each in two hours. Many we worked with were suffering from stress and anxiety. Some suffered from chronic aliments such as diabetes or chronic fatigue. Our focus was bringing compassionate attention and calm to each session, despite unforeseen interruptions, noises outside the treatment room, temperature changes in the room, clients missing appointments, etc.

One client reported that a long-held tightness in her left hip had released during the session, providing her immediate comfort. She was quite surprised because I didn't even place my hand on that hip. That experience provided an impetus for an abbreviated discussion on how Reiki works and the client pursuing Reiki training.

Each client received a feedback form with the option to be included on our mailing list. Over the course of the month, we saw over twenty clients, and all wished to be added to our list. Several have become clients and/or students outside of the office sessions.

What Jen and I learned from being able to offer Reiki within the office environment were several key points. For one, having an inside contact rather than cold calling made the job of convincing HR or the appropriate department of the merits of Reiki much easier. Having an organization like the Reiki Fellowship had created a pool of talented Reiki practitioners from which we were able to have that inside contact. We also learned that we needed to allow an extra ten minutes for each twenty-minute session due to clients running late from meetings and/or needing some extra time to discuss what they were feeling in the session or any questions they had about Reiki.

Incorporating Mobile Reiki Healing sessions into other venues holds tremendous potential. Businesses such as spas, medical offices, beauty salons, and events such as employee appreciation days can provide opportunities for introducing Reiki to the public.

In doing such outreach, it's helpful and advantageous to create a practitioner group, similar to the Reiki Fellowship, to provide ample support to handle the demands of the particular setting in which you are offering service. Having a group of other practitioners allows the tradeoff of shifts and the building of camaraderie and community with each outreach event. For a festival or exposition, a group of five to fifteen practitioners may be required, whereas a corporate service or one offered in a spa or other therapeutic setting might only need one or two practitioners.

Each outreach is an opportunity for the practitioner to market his or her services to the public. If a practitioner had to do this presentation alone, the costs of the festival entrance fee and booth equipment might be prohibitive. And one person would have difficulty handling all aspects of service at the booth—giving treatments, explaining Reiki to passersby, and everything else that needs to be done. With a group of practitioners, those who are more experienced at public speaking can take the "stage" and answer questions while others handle the business of scheduling and those who are more treatment-oriented give sample demonstrations. Practitioners can learn from each other, gain confidence working in different roles, and gain valuable practical experience in working with the public.

Thoughtful planning, careful scheduling, good equipment, proper dress, and being on time are all key factors in a successful outreach. The Reiki Fellowship had black and white T-shirts printed up with the slogans "Receive Your Reiki" to serve as a casual uniform for public outreaches. Even though we are individual practitioners, the T-shirts symbolize our cooperation under the umbrella of the Fellowship.

When we take Reiki out of the box and bring it to the world, we increase the number of people we can touch. So, get creative. If you can dream it, it can be done. Gather the resources and people you need, and as always, be prepared to be surprised!

Reiki for Veterans

After the US went to war in Iraq, families of deployed soldiers began coming to me for counseling and Reiki. Listening to the worries of parents and spouses and helping them to deal with their own fears, I realized that when these soldiers returned home, we would be seeing a new generation of PTSD (Post-Traumatic Stress Disorder) sufferers.

PTSD, the anxiety disorder that often occurs when an individual has been exposed to a traumatic event, is something veterans have often suffered in silence. Shutting away their combat experiences, they hope that the lingering feelings of confusion, fear, and anger will somehow disappear. Yet the numbness doesn't rid them of the problem. When they return to civilian life, they remain in a perpetual state of heightened alertness, which can be aggravated by the loss of the support of a structured military life. Many find a way to cope with this, stoically living with their fears, not letting on to others how they really feel. For some, more numbness is required. Left untreated, PTSD often manifests in unhealthy use of alcohol or drugs—anything that might help them numb their memories of the past. The tragedy of this route is how it numbs their present and future too, affecting their relationships with others, their jobs, their lives.

Knowing that Reiki has the effect of helping to unblock emotional obstacles and bring the mind, body, and spirit to balance, in 2004, I felt compelled to reach out to the local Veterans Center to see if there was a possibility of offering Reiki, either in session or class form.

Approaching the US Government was a daunting task. Back then, I had the impression that alternative care was not respected and did not know whether any other practitioners were offering this work to veterans. I conducted an Internet search and compiled the small amount of research material I found, wrote a cover letter, and sent healing energy to the project and to the initial meeting.

To my delight, I did get a response and a request to come and meet with staff. Passing through the doors of the Seattle Veteran's Center with the giant American eagle emblem hanging overhead, I was nervous, even though I felt charged with the presence of Reiki all around me. I inhaled deeply and went in to my first meeting. They received me courteously, although what most were really thinking, I had no idea. Then one of the administrative team, a counselor, leaned across to me and quietly informed me that he was actually a

Reiki Master and that he was pleased to see me. However, he went on, due to the limits of his job description, he was not able to cross the line and teach or practice Reiki with his clients.

This was the breakthrough I had hoped for. I felt that an opening had been created; I could breathe a little easier. But that was just the beginning. Over the course of the next couple of years, various staff from the Veteran's Center visited my training program and Reiki Circles, but we never seemed to get any closer to a program for veterans. Emails, correspondence, phone calls were all exchanged, but as time went on, the idea of implementing any kind of Reiki work with the veterans seemed little more than another well-intentioned pipe dream.

Then one day, after I had given up hope (perhaps had released attachment to result), I received a phone call, asking if I would be interested in teaching Reiki at the center as a volunteer. Timing is a funny thing though. After having held space for so long, that call came just as I was in the midst of a large life transition, which was to include my moving away from the Seattle area for an unknown length of time.

And that could have been the end of this tale, but for one of the Universe's happy "coincidences." As all of this was happening, a former student of mine, Michael Emanuel, by then a Reiki Master Teacher himself, came to a monthly Reiki Circle I held that was open to anyone interested in Reiki. He had not attended one of these for quite some time and only went that evening because about an hour before the circle started he felt a real need to go. The circle was much the same as others, except for two men, both complaining of significant physical pain and both on extensive medication. They were both in so much discomfort they had gathered the courage to see if Reiki could help relieve some of their symptoms. It did, though not in the way either man expected. These were short sessions, just twenty minutes, yet both men felt profoundly moved by their respective experiences. One of them said that he came to have his leg fixed and instead something big had shifted inside. Fighting to keep control of his emotions, he said he felt a calmness he hadn't felt in years, indeed since before he was in the first Gulf War. It was only then that we discovered they were both vets, and both were now interested in knowing if Reiki could help with their PTSD, a condition neither had mentioned before the session.

Michael was hooked. He now knew why he had needed to come to the circle that night. Early the next morning, he was on the phone to me to ask my views on whether we might be able to persuade the Department of Veterans Affairs to embrace Reiki. Perhaps even more than I had allowed myself to think, he felt convinced of the need to teach Reiki to veterans to become active participants in their own healing. I knew he was right, and now I knew who to hand the torch to as I was leaving Seattle.

In the months that followed, Michael worked with the Seattle Veterans Center and finally was able to get a Reiki I training day together, hosted at the Vet Center, supported by Vet Center staff, so veterans would be in familiar surroundings and only among other veterans. By now, my own life plans had changed again, and I was unexpectedly back in Seattle. So in November 2006, Michael and I set out to teach the first Reiki class. Ready as we could be for what we thought might be a very difficult day, with Vet Center counselors on hand in case of issues, we were both awestruck at the immediate effects that the healing energy of Reiki had on such a complicated and debilitating disorder. We had both had concerns about the difficulty of teaching Reiki to men trained for war. This was a self-selecting group of volunteers to be sure, but never had we encountered a group more energetically aware, or more willing to discuss, explore, and experiment with the possibilities of metaphysical energy. Far from facing difficulties, we left that day feeling wonderful with what we had accomplished and humbled by our clients.

It was not just that one class either. We have held others several times a year since, both Reiki I and Reiki II, and the reactions and results continue to amaze us. In each class, in the calm, restorative, and supportive atmosphere created, veterans voluntarily start sharing their feelings on their connection with the Reiki energy, many gently releasing long-held traumas in the form of stories and moments of intense personal insights.

We provide more for the veterans than only releasing and healing; in the classes we hold, we also encourage learning and experimenting, too. It became very clear to us early on that these guys are very much in touch with their instincts; it is part of their survival training. We have found our work, therefore, has also focused on helping them re-find what they already have—this time for "revival" rather than "survival." If at first I wasn't sure how open these men would be to working with *ki*, my concerns completely disappeared when, on our second class, Michael had a whole room of ex-marines and soldiers building up *ki* between their palms, exploring what it felt like, and then passing invisible bubbles of energy to one another and talking about what they were experiencing as they did.

As the only woman instructor, I was utterly honored to be amongst such genuine and open-hearted men, willing to share and discover how using Reiki could be such a powerful tool for their healing journeys. Here are just a few examples of what veterans have experienced while taking Reiki training with us.

> One veteran, Craig, looking up at the clock, noted that it was three in the afternoon. Without prompting, he shared with us how he had felt by this time every day for years: the screaming he felt inside, the rage he didn't always manage to control on the outside. Yet here it was, three o'clock on this Saturday, and he was perfectly relaxed, happy, and unbelievably calm. His sense of gratitude—even, as he said, if it was just for that day—was almost overwhelming.

> Another, Paul, was in tears during an attunement. Afterwards, he explained he had finally come to

know a place of peace within himself that he thought had left him long ago. He felt that by learning how to apply Reiki to himself he could actually begin to get a sense of "being quiet within" and that realization caused him much happiness, resulting in his tears of joy.

We have yet to work with a veteran who has not been able to work with Reiki. Although some have needed follow-up sessions to get confidence that they really can feel Reiki, and several have not continued with the work, most realize almost immediately that they are able to "feel" the energy of Reiki as buzzing, heat, movement, connection.

Jesse had been trained in special operations to become aware of his auric field so that he could perceive when an attacker was nearby. During the course of the Reiki training, he was able for the first time to go into a relaxed state when one of us came near his field to do a treatment or attunement. He explained that it wasn't easy to just let go of the ability to be on alert, but he explained that by the end of the workshop he was learning a new way of dealing with people approaching him—a core fundamental of Reiki practice; the ability to sense a person's intention. This distinguishing feature allowed Jesse's hyper-vigilance to soften enough when sensing a healing intention approaching versus an intruding one.

But probably the most amazing and dramatic effect of the Reiki training was Mark's spontaneous healing story.

During the afternoon of a Reiki I class, Mark shared how his long-term leg pain from shrapnel wounds had all but disappeared during the second Reiki attunement. After the attunement, he disappeared to another room for a few minutes to be by himself. When he came back into the room, he wanted to share with us what he had just experienced. He described how he felt an immense darkness lifted from him during the attunement. It was, he said, like an intensely black slab floating out of him. He then told us how it had descended over thirty years earlier when he was just one of fifteen out of his entire company to survive a firefight in Vietnam. What struck us most was Mark's incredible composure and grace as he told us his story and his experience of the attunement just minutes before. He finished by saying he would never forget the moment when the darkness descended or his comrades that didn't make it, but that his life had just changed for the better, and he knew the black slab that had floated from him was never coming back. In an email to Michael following his Reiki I training he wrote:

It was a most interesting and beneficial day. I'm still reflecting on my personal experiences during the attunement. And ... I wanted to pass on an overview of my pain relief results for the day. In that regard, the nerve pain in my right leg (related to a couple of old shrapnel wounds) has recently made it very hard to drive for any length of time, to sit in a chair for long, or to even sleep at night. Normally, sitting or driving will send me straight into searing pain and frequently into strong nerve flashes. Once this gets going, the only solution is multiple doses of VA prescribed pain meds. ...

The day of the Reiki [Level 1 training] session, I drove for almost two hours to get there, spent much of the session in a chair, and then drove another hour and a

*half home. Normally this would be an almost impos-
sible task with this leg problem. I took one pain pill
early in the Reiki session ("one" is never enough to
do much for my leg). But ... somehow ... through the
benefits of you, Eileen, and Reiki, I made it all the
way though the rest of the session, all the way home,
and through the night without any other pills. That
has not happened in months, and I consider it to be
nothing short of a miracle. I'm still scratching my
head as to how Reiki works. But ... somehow it did
does something positive for me. And ... for that, my
sincerest "thank you" to both you and Eileen!*

The Reiki work with the veterans has really just begun. But
the government is beginning to be interested in alternative care to
help the veterans.

.As more and more awareness grows of the benefits of Reiki
on PTSD and healing injuries, offering Reiki sessions or classes to
our local VA will become easier and more accepted, and beneficial
for all involved.

Bringing Universal Energy to the Main Stage

My desire for acting had been with me for a long time. Growing
up in northern New Jersey, I often went into New York City to see
Broadway shows and was always envious of the dancers and actors.
But my family's wishes typified many, to discourage pursuing acting as a profession because it was perceived to be something you
could not really make a living at. So instead, I went to college and
then graduate school and became a professional career counselor.

But all through that journey, the creative muse in me would beg
for attention. I gave it space in a lot of forms—mainly in creating
the healing practice and school, but occasionally through writing,
drawing, and painting.

Finally, after fifteen years of working as a counselor, I took the leap and fulfilled that long-time dream of entering acting school to pursue becoming an actor. I had reached a place in my life many others experience on the Reiki journey—unleashing yet another aspect of their full potential.

I felt very guided into the Seattle Acting School. When I watched my first class, the instructor sounded like a spiritual teacher rather than acting coach. He emphasized being in the moment and trusting the flow. He even could sense where the other actors were holding back in expressing themselves.

That instructor turned out to be JD Coburn who had studied with the late Sanford Meisner, a pioneer in American acting tradition. Mr. Coburn was trained to teach acting in a way similar to how we are trained to practice Reiki: by taking part in a disciplined approach to the craft that is handed down from master teacher to master teacher. Mr. Meisner passed on his tradition of acting to Bob Carnegie, noted director, and Carnegie passed the tradition on to Mr. Coburn.

I found that as I embraced the techniques handed down by Meisner, I began to practice acting the way I had always practiced Reiki: being in the here and now, letting go of the ego, responding to what was in front of me with an open heart, and not being attached to the result of my efforts. In the beginning of our acting studies, an emphasis on listening and responding and staying in the moment is crucial to building the groundwork to be able to express ourselves spontaneously on the stage. The basic idea is that you yourself are enough as an actor. Now be that. Or as my mentor JD would say, "Do that now."

This was the foundation for my first year of training. During that time, I continued to teach Reiki at my school, and several of the actors who were in my acting class expressed interest in healing arts and began to study with me also. It was an incredible experience, witnessing my artistic colleagues exploring their own spiritual truths. Not only did we have the language of the stage as common ground, but we also began to incorporate Universal Energy into that dialogue.

Just as within the Reiki community, the actors themselves came from a wide variety of backgrounds and traditions of all ages.

Half the acting class eventually learned either Reiki Level 1 or 2 from me, and it wasn't uncommon to see some of the actors with their hands over their heart or solar plexus in preparation before going on stage.

One Reiki acting colleague, Richard Scott, put it this way about how he saw Reiki and acting:

> Acting first and foremost involves working in an imaginary circumstance. For that it's completely different from any other work you can do, especially Reiki. And for that reason, acting does not apply to Reiki in any way that the average person thinks it might. In fact, I would say that trying to "act" in your Reiki sessions as a practitioner would be downright dangerous. Most people think acting is about putting on a show, and so it might be tempting to think an actor who does Reiki might walk into the room and "pretend" to feel what the patient is feeling or to just "look like you care." Nothing could be farther from the truth, however, about acting or Reiki. If you've got some crazy idea about acting, you can downright hurt your fellow actors. The same is true with Reiki. If you've tried to get attunements off the Internet or have avoided learning under a good Reiki master, you can mislead your patients.

In the second year of training, we were introduced to a technique called "emotional preparation." The actor imagines him- or herself in various emotionally charged situations (either very angry, depressed, or happy) and living out the feelings truthfully as he or she begins the scene on stage. Emotional preparation was and is the most challenging technique to work with in my course of study. You deliberately bring on an intense emotional state, which can leave your energy field feeling quite wired before and after.

Another one of my Reiki acting colleagues, Tom Brophy, put it this way:

> When I started to prepare [emotionally] for such moments, I found I would get intense anxiety (albeit somewhat helpful to the role, but it didn't help me to relax and get focused to do the work). The result was the anxiety made me incoherent and I, more often than not, would lose focus in my objective in the scene. But, when it was suggested to me by my Reiki teacher to try using Reiki before my preparations, it worked great.
>
> Reiki and acting are a perfect combination. Both are done instinctually and provide the best work when done through the heart chakra. What an incredible complement to the acting problem. Not only was I able to relax better during my preparations, but also I was able to retain my focus for the duration of the scene, which helped give clarity to the words I was reciting, getting a better connection with my working partner (fellow actor) and to the emotional depth that went along with the words. I found that it made my work all the more truthful. In addition to utilizing Reiki before preparations, I found I would give myself Reiki after these particularly emotional scenes to smooth out my energy field and to get myself grounded again in this reality and to enable me to let go more freely any residual negative emotional angst.

I had a similar experience. As I eventually attended auditions, and after years of being the "good witch" as a Reiki master, I was not surprisingly cast as that in a local production of *The Wizard of Oz*. But I also wanted to explore the opposite polarity, so I put my desire to the Universe. A few days later, there was a cancellation in the cast, and they also asked me to be the wicked witch, and I could feel the joy that comes from freedom of expression!

Eventually I was cast as an ensemble performer in *Tony and Tina's Wedding*, the off-Broadway production that comes to town each year. I played another polarity figure from my Reiki master self. In this production, I was the floozy dancer girlfriend to the groom's father. Think of the girls at Tony Soprano's nightclub. Not at all Reiki realm!

I find using Reiki as a self-treatment helps me to go in and out of character, especially when it is often so foreign to my day-to-day existence.

Richard Scott also had this to say:

> Solving the acting problem provides a person with empathy skills that can also translate to Reiki. When practicing Reiki, you are allowing a person's innermost feelings to tell the truth about what they're feeling or experiencing. So, you have to be able to look at a person, try to understand what's going on under the surface, and be able to empathize without judgment. It's a skill that many suppress in their lives and one that acting forces you to master. That's good for any Reiki practitioner. And that's why it's so important to study Reiki under a competent Reiki master— one who understands something about the human condition. The master has a deep responsibility in this regard. Like the acting coach, the Reiki master must give students a safe space to practice in and refine their skill—a place to safely make mistakes and break what they came to accept as convention before starting their training.

After almost two years of training, I kept getting the impression that I wanted to merge the two disciplines of Reiki and acting together, not just in using the healing technique to calm distress or align in manifesting roles. I wasn't sure what it would look like, but I "held space."

In my first effort toward that goal, I gained the confidence to do my own recording of meditation CDs for my students.

Then, in my third year of pursuing acting, an opportunity came that began to fulfill that greater vision. I became the artistic director of a show that had been started by two writers only in the previous year called the Seattle Cold Readers. Local play writers and screenwriters would submit their scripts, and actors would read them in front of a live audience. With all the connections I had made in acting school, especially of those actors who had trained in Reiki, I knew we could take this show to the next level.

Fast forward to now. The Seattle Cold Readers has become a one-of-a-kind show, still incorporating the scripts and actors, but adding variety talent, such as dancers and singers, into the mix. We choose scripts for their unique content. Some explore spiritual themes, such as cults or magic. Others are more traditional dramas. And some are outright hilarious comedies.

As my script supervisor and I are both Reiki masters, we are quite sensitive to the energies that come through the various scripts we select for each show. Sometimes writers have such great attachment to their stories that they have a difficult time editing material to fit our show. We'll often send Reiki to help facilitate the process, as always, for the highest good. Other times, the synergy isn't there, and similar to what happens in working with energy, that which does not serve falls away, and the writers take their scripts elsewhere.

The basics of our training, "working off the other actor," "reacting to what is in front of you," and what I would call "Reiki Theater," or trusting the flow of a scene, are all put forth into an enjoyable and unforgettable production. Since several of the actors selected for each show are also Reiki practitioners, they transmit the healing energy through their lines and actions with each other. Not only are audience members captivated by quality acting and engaging dialogue, but they are also receiving the flow of Reiki as it transmits from each actor and the Cold Readers Team who support and hold space for the show. Before each show, all the members of the Seattle Cold Readers team, who are all advanced Reiki practitioners, send positive light to the space in which we perform and to the cast, crew, and talent.

Our shows have been charging the audience in a very dramatic and uplifting manner. In addition, Seattle Cold Readers has been featured on public access TV, and we have had our story printed in our city's art's magazine. There is nothing like live theater for energizing the soul! We also give unknown writers a chance to be heard and an opportunity to see their own work read live.

Since I wear the hat of artistic director, most patrons are surprised to learn that my day job is being a Reiki master. I enjoy the reactions—and giving evidence of possibilities made real— when I explain what I do to others because people perceive both pursuits, Reiki and acting, as dream jobs. I have always believed in the adage that if you can dream it you can manifest it. And, as I explained earlier, I've had the dream of being an actor and a healer since my childhood.

Combining these two disciplines into the Seattle Cold Readers show is like experimenting in a living laboratory each time we perform. How can we adjust the sound, the lighting so the audience will be able to take in that much more of what we present? What about creating Reiki stand-up comedy? Or a short play on Reiki? Over the years I've also been involved as an extra in various feature films, and in each instance, I have introduced cast and crew to Reiki while on set.

So for all you other creative artists and actors out there, I encourage the exploration into both Reiki and your art and seeing how it will begin to influence those around you. Take Reiki to the stage, screen, and beyond. Perhaps a motion picture will be made. Take Reiki out of the box and see where it will take you!

Healing the Waters with Reiki

This is a story of the convergence of healers, healing intention, and helping the planet by surrendering to something greater than one's self and gently holding space for what will occur.

The Duwamish River blessings the Reiki Fellowship became involved in begins with the work of Dr. Masura Emoto, who has photographed the effect of healing intention and positive versus negative words on the crystalline structure of water. When he was coming to Seattle on a speaking engagement, his coordinator asked me if I would facilitate healing blessings of various areas of water in the Seattle, as Dr. Emoto was leading other blessings for the Puget Sound.

The Reiki Fellowship initially held two simultaneous blessings: one in the north part of the city at Green Lake Park and the other at the south end at the Duwamish River.

The Duwamish served as a main artery through the Puget Sound for the Native Americans before the settlers came. Once white settlement came to the Sound, industry cropped up along the river, and in the last century, much of the river had become so polluted it was declared a Superfund site.

After the first blessing we did, the Boeing company, whose factory over the years had contributed much of the pollutants to the river, announced it was going to offer two million dollars for a cleanup to begin next year. So, we decided to repeat the blessings each month. Dr. Emoto was encouraging other healers and community members around the world to continue the process each month for six months and then take a water sample to see the final effect.

Dr. Emoto doesn't consider his work science, but art, and I thought, being an artist myself, if all else, it would contribute to art, to community building, and possibly to the health of the river. It then occurred to me that other members of the community might also be interested in contributing their gifts of song, music, and healing abilities, and I opened the circle wider.

Enter the next phase of our blessing ceremony, where Rose De Dan of Wild Reiki and Shamanic Healing and Leslie Britt, another colleague in shamanism, brought their gifts of ritual to open each ceremony. Then, Sha'ari Garfinkel of Inner Listening joined our crew, offering her gift of the healing power of sound. All women were called to work with the healing of the Duwamish for years prior to our convergence. At the beginning of each ceremony, both Rose and Leslie have welcomed the energies of each direction and have led us into ritual and song of the Earth Mother, Pachamama. We, then, blow our intentions into sacred cedar that is passed around the group. Sha'ari takes cedar healing intentions and merges them with water from the river in her beautiful crystal bowl, which she plays, sending out the vibrations across the park into the Duwamish below. As the cedar is released into the great river, participants send Reiki and thoughts to the water. Sha'ari has played beautiful Native American flute for our contemplation, and in other events, some of us have played bells and gongs and joined in toning "om." Each time we have done this, flocks of geese have come over to our group along the shore to take in the energy we were generating as well as to be carriers for the blessing as they floated back out along the river.

Finishing with the statements Dr. Emoto has said to bodies of water everywhere, "I love you, I thank you, and I respect you," we then close the ceremony as it was opened, honoring the directions and coming back into our centers of truth.

As we have just begun our collaborations to affect the health of the river, the results of our efforts are still forthcoming. But since we have begun, radio press, our local National Public Radio station, has conducted an interview about our work.

What I have noticed in becoming more public in my approach to healing, however, is that, although a Reiki practitioner may come with good intentions, the process of change is not an easy one for all to embrace. After the blessing where we sang the Pachamama song, Rose received much criticism from her shamanic community of spreading a sacred song into the public who had not been initiated into the tradition from which it came. It is interesting to note that effect because, on the one hand, holding songs and rituals sacred does keep their energy intact with source. On the other hand, releasing them out into the world, for the purpose of healing, allows for the effects to spread even further.

But perhaps with conflict can come resolution. Just like the conflict in the river that had to be declared openly before monies and resources could start being applied to help in its clean up, so too, this disagreement needed public airing before we could settle it. And, in a similar way, I have felt compelled to bring Reiki out into the world that all may benefit.

Overall, the process of the Duwamish blessings has reminded me of all the Reiki work I have done and continue to do:

- Gathering people together to participate in classes, circles, and sessions;

- Developing the healing technique of Insight Reiki, which came out of my training and background as a counselor;

- Taking Reiki out into various environments, corporate, theater, and outdoors and delving into working with veterans on their own healing.

It's just a beginning in touching the world through Reiki.

Many other practitioners around the world have brought Reiki into healthcare settings, conducted research, developed other integrated methods to further the technique. I feel if the founder of the system, Mikao Usui, could have witnessed the evolution of how far Reiki has come since its humble beginnings, he would be proud.

I hope the gatherings I have facilitated, those I continue to organize, and this book will inspire individuals to carry this work beyond their personal experience. With their raised consciousness, others can create their own healing gatherings and get involved at their local level to initiate change to their environment, community, and the world.

I pass the work on to you.

Reiki Guided Meditations

I have written and recorded the following guided meditations. You may purchase them through www.reikitrainingprogram.com.

Permission to Receive: Reiki Journeys for Self Discovery & Healing

Reiki Treatment for Self

Allow this Reiki self-treatment to be a time for you to go within. Free yourself from distractions, turning the phone off, dimming the lights, lying down or sitting comfortably. You may want to light a candle or burn some incense to soften the mood around you.

Now, when you are ready, take a moment. Give yourself permission to receive this session.

Connect in with your breath and notice how you feel.

Scan your body from the top of your head to the tips of your toes and notice any areas where you are holding on. Gently breathe into these areas and allow the breath to open these spaces up. Where the breath goes, the Reiki flows.

Notice how that feels.

Now, with your **int**ention to give yourself Reiki, bring your **att**ention to your hands.

Bring them up to cover your eyes. Gently, your fingers are cupped and you lay your hands upon your face with a light touch. Fingers together. Lightly letting your hands cover your eyes and effortlessly allowing the energy to flow, bathing and nurturing all that your eyes see and take in on a daily basis.

Notice how good that feels. Taking the time to nurture your eyes.

Each hand position we go through covers the chakras, the energy centers of your being.

Between your eyes on your forehead is your third eye, your sixth chakra.

This is the area where you see beyond what is there, you tap into your intuition, you see what is real. It's a place of deep understanding and connection. As you bring your hands there, you are bringing light and energy to assist in clearing this space so you can see and intuit clearly.

The sixth chakra is connected to the seventh chakra, located above, on the crown of your head connecting you to the Universal life force, to the creative essence that is within you and all around you.

With your hands over your eyes, just allowing the Universal life force of Reiki to flow through the top of your head, down through your eyes, infusing the rest of your body and mind with radiant light energy.

Notice how that feels.

Now, moving your hands to cover your ears and the top part of your jaw, hold your face tenderly in your hands. Feel how good it is to cradle your face, giving soothing energy to your jaw, for all the talking, chewing, and swallowing you do each and every day.

Your jaw takes in the support of your hands, of the Reiki energy. Feel that support.

Now, nurture your ears, for they too, like your eyes, take in so much information, sounds, conversations, nuances throughout the day.

These hand positions are excellent if you feel yourself coming down with a cold, or if you have a headache, or if you just need some quiet time, some relief, an immediate sanctuary.

Right here in your hands.

Each hand position should be held for one to three minutes, enough time to let the energy begin to flow effortlessly. There may be occasions where you want to let your hands rest upon you for ten minutes or more.

You will begin to trust your intuition the more that you work with Reiki on yourself and others.

Now, from your ears, move your hands so that they are covering your neck and throat.

You may find it more comfortable to hold the sides of your neck or to put one hand over the other in front of your throat.

Let yourself flow with whatever is most comfortable.

Ease into this space.

It's so important to be comfortable when giving oneself Reiki. The energy opens up and flows that much more strongly.

Relax into your throat, take a breath there. Notice what you notice. How does this area feel now that you have your hands over your throat? This is your fifth chakra, the energy center of self-expression. How do you give voice in the world? How do speak your truth? Notice the sensation in your hands as you give yourself Reiki to this area as well as to all the other areas that we give this self-treatment.

There is no wrong or right in doing Reiki. There just is.

Now, gently letting your hands move down from your throat to cover your heart, hand above hand, hand over hand, or fingertips touching each other across the chest.

It doesn't matter how you do the hand positions on your self or the exact form; it's more important to bring intention for healing with the attention of your hands.

Letting yourself relax into giving your heart this endless supply of energy.

Reiki flows through the crown of your head down your body through your heart and out the chakras of your palms.

As you give to your heart, you are creating a continuous circuit of Universal Love.

Inhale this circuit.

Let yourself be surrounded and suffused in it.

The heart is the fourth chakra, the energy center where we give and receive love.

Letting ourselves be loved. Effortlessly. Letting the energy in to help heal those parts of our heart where we've been hurt, where we hold back.

Letting our heart heal from past wounds and emerge, renewed and refreshed with radiant light.

Letting this light shine forth from the center of our being so that all whom we interact with receive the blessings of love.

Giving Reiki to my heart helps me fall asleep peacefully and also allows me to come into a very centered state quickly. It's a useful hand position for meditation.

Notice what you notice now about your heart area.

How does it feel different from when we first started? Be curious.

Now, moving the hands down the chest to cover the abdomen, the area of our third chakra, our solar plexus. This is the fire in our belly. The will and drive to get things done. The center of our being, the inner knowing of our sensitive intestines, lined with so much of our intuitive nervous system. This area needs a lot of Reiki in most people. We spend the bulk of our days doing, doing, doing. Consuming, consuming. Our third chakra often just needs a time-out. It needs a lot of energy and support to keep functioning properly.

It also needs balancing with the heart chakra, so you can experiment with putting one hand on the heart and the other over the belly and notice how that feels. These two hand placements are another soothing way to fall asleep or to begin a meditation. Very centering, very grounding.

Spending time here, breathing into your hands, breathing into these chakras. Feel how good it is to relax and be supported here.

Reiki flows through the body, from the front into the back. Notice as I say this how your back begins to feel. Those tense places in the shoulders or the low back now open to receive extra support, extra energy, effortlessly from your hands on the front of your being. The Reiki energy dissolves through you, within you, to the back. Imagine this warm cocoon of energy supporting the front and back of your being. Rest here for a while.

Now, gently moving our hands and our attention to the top of our pelvis, our lower abdomen. Just letting the Reiki effortlessly flow into the second chakra, the energy center of our passion, our creativity, our connection to our family. Our pelvis is connected to the skeletal system of our body, our underlying foundation. The pelvis encircles the base of our being. A perfect cauldron for the passionate fire that burns within us. Letting the energy flow to support that skeleton, flowing down into the sacrum, the sacred bone of our spine. Breathing here, resting here.

Now move the hands out to the hips. Notice how moving the hands to the bony areas of the body feels different from the soft tissue. Our root chakra, at the base of our spine extends down and out through our hips and our legs. Our root is the foundation of our being, our connection to abundance, to the earth. Our legs are like extensions that reach downward and connect us to that earthly flow. Feel the energy radiating downward and through the legs.

If it feels right, move the hands down to cover the knees, the places where we bend and flex and move through the world. Giving gratitude for the knees, the joints, our legs. For all they do, for how they support us and move us through life. And allowing the energy to flow effortless from the knees down through the ankles and feet. If you are seated, you can bend over and touch the tops of the ankles or feet. If you are lying down, just feeling your hands and the energy that emanate from them extending down and out and through.

Scanning yourself again from the top of your head through the tips of your toes and noticing now that the sensation of energy is like flowing through the front and back of your being. The places that still require a bit more opening, allow your breath to fill in those spaces. Resting, breathing, centering into the fullness of this experience. You can even allow your energy field now to expand out in a bubble all around you. Your aura, filling with radiant light that is suffusing your entire being.

Then with your hands, gently smoothing out your auric field from the top of your head to the tips of your toes, smoothing away any energy blocks that have become dissolved and beginning to bring to a close this wonderful healing session. All sessions, whether given to oneself or others must have a beginning, middle, and end. The beginning starts with our intention, the middle is the treatment, and the end is the smoothing of the aura.

When you are done, bring your palms together as if in prayer, or Namaste. Take a few breaths and being to slowly, gently bring yourself out of the treatment. Or, if you are taking this treatment into your sleep, allow yourself to drift off effortlessly, letting the rest of the words I say float around you as you drift softly into sleep.

Now, notice what has changed since we began.

Notice which areas are still taking their time opening up and giving themselves permission to receive.

Notice what you notice, be curious. There is no diagnosis, just presence each and every time you give yourself Reiki. It is an exercise in self-healing and in self-witnessing. It is an exercise to strengthen the intuition and to provide a foundation for daily discoveries of energy. You can perform this self-treatment in parts, the top of the body in the morning, the lower half in the evening. You can also do the treatment fully at the end of the day and be guided off into sleep. Experiment. Be open to trying different sequences. Find what works for you. Develop trust in your own ability as a healer. Walk the path with an open mind.

Cosmic Reiki

Let yourself get comfortable.

Focus on your breathing and settle in to where you are seated or lying down.

If you are attuned to the distant symbol, bring this into your crown now.

Take a few deep breaths. Begin to cultivate a curious mind and let the right side of your brain, where your creative imagination comes forth from, start to stretch and expand.

Settle into this place of expansion with each breath.

Now, scan your being from the top of your head to the tips of your toes.

Notice what you notice. Expand those areas of your being that still feel a little tight, bringing your breath and any Reiki symbols into these areas, giving them time and space so that they can gently release.

First, sensing ourselves within our body, scanning head to toe.

Being with what is there, not fixing, not changing, just noticing. Noticing thoughts, feelings, and impressions

Soothing, settling in, you are now prepared to go on a journey.

With the powers of your creative mind, you expand your sense of self so that you are hovering ever so slightly just above the physical body and into the space of your aura.

Scanning from head to toe in this auric field, taking your time and noticing any changes here at this level, what thoughts, feelings, impressions draw your curiosity.

Just taking note.

Anything that begins to draw your awareness or curiosity, begin to zoom in a bit. Get closer to the phenomena and breathe into the focus, expanding and opening it into a new place.

As each area unfolds, let the flow of the experience guide you to the next place.

Now, expanding out even further from the aura, to about a foot around you. Notice this feeling, what you perceive here. Scan down through your field from about a foot from the top of your head to a foot below your feet. Sense this cocoon of energy you are in and notice any thoughts, feelings, or impressions here.

Be curious. Breathing into anything that draws your awareness and makes you curious.

Spend time and allow the process to unfold.

From this expanded state, expand even further, now sensing yourself filling up the entire room you are in. Breathe into how far your own energy field can go.

Notice how you are able to go through the walls of your room and up through the ceiling into the room above. Keep going up until you gently come through the roof of the building in which you are in. From this place, look down through all the layers at your own being resting below. Spend a few moments here in this perspective.

Now, stretching upward, expand yourself so that you are out into the sky. Notice the feeling of the air, the clouds, and the sun if its day or the moon if it is evening. Feel your own sense merging with this greater field, the atmosphere. Stretching even further, you move above the sky to the outer reaches of the atmosphere and begin to move into the vastness of space.

Spend a few moments here, getting acquainted with this vastness that is within you and without you.

Feel your being encircling the planet below … in a protective layer of love …

Wider now, your arms reach out around the globe.

Reiki is the vibration of the void. Reiki is the material manifestation of the void. It is the vibration that emits from the void. When you give yourself permission to receive Reiki at a deeper level, you give yourself permission to go back into the void or allow the void to come up and meet you, to become more open and not consume or fill in.

See your home, Earth, as if it were a ball, and you, as a child, are now holding it in your hand …

As you look at it, you feel the connection you share with this blue-green orb ... mother, Gaia, home.

Now, also notice the other planets and stars around you ... in you ... part of you ...

Turning outward now, you leave Earth behind and breathe in the celestial bodies of this solar system ... as they pass through you and you through them ... feeling connected ...

Further on, you see out beyond the Milky Way ...

Breathe in the vastness of this space ... in and out ... endless. Breathe in this sense of infinity, limitless. Breathe out your own being, stretching it into the dark, rich blackness that you are now swimming in.

Floating through, you encounter a rainbow bridge of light ... This bridge transports you to a heavenly, angelic realm ... Breathe in and feel for yourself the presence of guides and sages there to guide you on your path towards Source ...

Notice your surroundings ... focus on your breathing ... in and out ...

Feel the love around you, in you, as you go further inward towards your Divine Light ...

Feel yourself merging now, bright cosmic radiance of your being ...

The eternal you ... the you that knows all answers ...

Feel free to ask this part of you any questions now ... any question that has been on your mind ... allowing your self to digest this and patiently come forth with an answer ...

Feel the power of this Source coming in between your eyes, where your third eye would be ... Allow yourself to breathe in this energy, of all knowledge and power ...

Listen/see/hear/sense what your answer may be ...

If no answer comes, give thanks to this higher aspect of you and know that at any time you can access this place where your answers lie ...

Once again ... feel free to float ... back down through the angelic realms ...

Giving thanks to the sages and guides that are also part of you,
work with you whenever you call upon them for assistance ...
gliding across the rainbow bridge ... back out into the Milky Way ...
You feel yourself being drawn back through this solar system,
coming down to your home, Earth.
You now understand your attraction to this planet ...
why you are here now, at this time.
Coming further down, through the atmosphere, the sky ...
the trees ... this building ...
into your crown, feeling the Divine energy pulsing, rotating,
above your head,
containing all knowledge, all power of your being ...
This energy then moves down through your body ... coming down
Your throat, your heart ... Feel it pulsing there ... your belly ...
going down your spine ... and legs ... grounding down into
the earth.
Feel yourself elongate into the earth ...
Feel yourself supported by this land, as your feet stretch into
the ground ...
Allow Earth energy to now swirl around you, coming up
through you roots, coming up from the heart of the planet ...
through your feet, your legs, the base of your spine.
your belly, your heart ... Allow it to swirl within the heart
as you now open to the celestial energies streaming through
your crown and feel these energies mixing, converging,
becoming one within the vessel of your heart ... breathing in,
expanding the volume of light and love ... breathing in
even further.
Allow yourself to radiate this light.
Notice how good it feels.
Notice how effortlessly it pours forth from your being.
This journey through the cosmos
back to the center of your being,
now revitalized,

refreshed,
renewed,
to take in the next new moment
and shine forth as the Light that you are ...

Sharing My Heart: Guided Meditations to Expand Heart-centered Consciousness

Awakened Heart

Close your eyes.
> Connect to your breath.
> Feel the rhythm in and out.
> Gentle flow,
> Nurturing, nourishing, bringing you quietly to your center.
> Feeling the ebb and flow of breath, your lungs expanding

and contracting,
> your heart pumping the blood through your veins and arteries,
> the oxygen you inhale charging and cleansing your blood with
> the energy of the Universe.
> Inhaling Reiki as it flows all through your circulation
> and coming back and through the powerful pump of your heart,
> this place of life-giving,
> this center of your being.
> Each beat is an offering of love to the rest of your body
> and to the whole Universe.
> You become the beat.
> You become the whole
> through the portal of your heart.
> Each chamber a sacred space for the alchemical transforma-

tion of your blood into
> the fluid of liquid love and light.
> Feeling this liquid light flowing through your body
> from head to toe,

surrounded and supported in love

as your being feels nurtured by the essence of the Universe,

your heart begins expanding, and the pulsing and pumping of love begins to surround and infuse your aura with light and adoration.

Brilliant luminescence expanding outward beyond the boundaries of your self,

the light of love reaches out around to fill the entire room you are sitting in.

Fill this space complete with this light.

Then effortlessly, expanding beyond the walls outside, beyond the roof, the grounds, out into the neighborhood,

the town or city you are in and infusing light into the spaces that most need healing,

letting your creative imagination expand and see and feel the light being offered with the gentlest of ease to those who most require it at this time,

perhaps it's groups of people or certain individuals you know

or animals, plants, or other aspects of the environment.

Trust your inner knowing. Give some space if no direction appears.

Using your imagining inner vision.

Release attachment to the results of your offering.

letting go of the need to have an effect,

to just be in the flow.

Pulsing through you and out through the sacredness of your heart.

radiance, beauty, joy glow,

beaming light and love.

Seeing all those surrounded in the glow becoming nurtured and healed by this offering.

breathing in and out.

deeply satisfied,

gratified

by this heart offering.

Begin to gently and slowly draw back your awareness into the space of the room you are in, and notice now how this room has changed in quality.

Sit in the space of this awareness.

Breathe deeply.

Relax into the being of giving,

coming back into yourself further,

feeling the inhale and exhale of your breath,

noticing what you notice in your being now.

Scanning from head to toe, be in the space of this awareness.

And gently, coming back into the awareness of the center of your being,

to the graciousness of your heart,

your life, your love,

your own beautiful expression of the unique being that is YOU!

Expanded Heart

With your heart now open and inspired, return to a safe space for the exploration of thoughts and feelings and the expression of tears, joy, and laughter, a place where you won't be disturbed and can be free to express whatever emotion requires you to release.

As you daydream and get comfortable, give yourself permission to feel your breath and the beating of your heart fully within.

I encourage you to allow even more space for your breath, to become even that much more comfortable within the rhythm of your being.

Let your mind drift to different events that have happened over your life that have brought you joy. Fond memories, shared intimacies, playful exchanges, laughter.

Begin to focus in on the laughter memories.

Like coming in close with a telephoto lens, you zoom in towards the events that brought such poignant humor to your heart.

Perhaps it was a situation that caught you off guard and took you by surprise. Perhaps it was something you did to yourself accidentally.

Let this unexpected, unanticipated event have more room to expand within your being so that you have a full-body recollection of the experience and the silliness, the absurdity that overtook you in that moment.

Give yourself permission to fully feel the laughter related to this event. Let yourself relax into the laughter, letting it build amongst other memories and other thoughts related or otherwise.

Perhaps the thoughts become even a bit more absurd or unreal and change into hypothetical scenes that couldn't possibly occur but yet keep building upon the laughter before.

Let your imagination have permission to become wild!

Think to yourself what if..., and let your imagination fill in the details.

Let yourself and your full being become saturated with the humor and recollection of this moment.

With the fullness of impossibility and amusement ...

this amusement heals. It heals the heart, the mind, the body and soul.

It allows for your breath to be fully absorbed through your heart and your consciousness to come into a deeper understanding of your truth.

Take lots of time here.

Let the process evolve rather than be forced from within, coming from the humor, from the heart, that extends deep with the source of this laughter.

Let the awareness in your heart expand to be saturated with the fullness of this humor

like a sponge absorbing the laughter, the tears, the recollections,

each wave cleansing out your heart, making more and more room for you to go even that much deeper into the humor.

Let yourself go and be held in the wave of laughter.

Experience it full body, full mind, completely. Take all the time you need here,

letting each memory begin to yield to an awareness of your present place in space,

each breath bringing you closer back to center.

Become aware of the transformation that has occurred in your being at this time.

All your cells, all yourself nurtured anew in the heart bath of sacred laughter.

Feel renewed and revitalized in this energy that has now permeated your being, your journey toward

an awakened heart!

Reiki Links and Bibliography

Internet Connections

The Artist's Way
www.theartistsway.com
For those just beginning their creative journey as well as those restarting their artistic engines.

Emoto Peace Project
www.geocities.jp/emotoproject/english/about.html
Organization to give away Dr. Emoto's book, *The Message from Water*, to all the children of the world to promote enlightenment and peace.

Inner Listening
www.inner-listening.com
Sha'ari Garfinkel's mission of inner listening is to create physical, emotional, and spiritual health through the application of time-honored music therapies and counseling.

International Association of Reiki Practitioners
www.iarpreiki.org
Connecting Reiki practitioners from around the world, offering a newsletter and zip code look-up of practitioners in your region. Also offers liability insurance for Reiki practitioners.

International Center for Reiki Training
www.reiki.org
Founded by William Lee Rand, is a portal for Reiki articles, *Reiki News Magazine*, links to Reiki research articles, classes, and more.

The One Gathering
www.theonegathering.com
The annual event in Seattle, Washington, whose mission is to expand and lift consciousness to promote peace and joy.

The Reiki Digest
http://reikidigest.blogspot.com/
A free online publication offering cutting edge stories about Reiki in the world.

Reiki Fellowship
www.reikifellowship.com
"Connecting the World with Reiki" offers Reiki practitioners, teachers, and students on the path an opportunity to do outreach in their communities and participate in events that spread Reiki consciousness.

Reiki Training Program
www.reikitrainingprogram.com
For more information on Eileen Dey, additional copies of this book, as well as the Insight Reiki guided meditation CD and other guided meditation CDs to assist the Reiki practitioner on his or her path. Also, the only state-licensed vocational school of Reiki offering both practitioner and master programs.

Wild Reiki and Shamanic Healing
www.reikishamanic.com
Rose De Dan is a paq'o and mesa carrier in the Q'ero Peruvian
Andean medicine tradition, considered to be one of the last unbro-
ken shamanic lineages in the world today. She is also an animal
communicator, Reiki Master Teacher, author, and artist.

Hands-on Healing Bibliography

The Artist's Way: A Spiritual Path to Higher Creativity
    by Julia Cameron

The Complete Book of Traditional Reiki
    by Amy Z. Roland

Creating the Work You Love
    by Rick Jarow

Essential Reiki
    by Diane Stein

The Gift of Reiki
    by Susan Bradford, Claudia Fischer and Catherine Roche

Hands of Light
    by Barbara Ann Brennan

*The Medicine Woman's Guide to Being in Business for Yourself: How
    to Live by Your Spiritual Vision in a Money-Based World*
    by Carol Bridges

Reiki for Dummies
    by Nina L. Paul

The Therapeutic Touch: How to Use Your Hands to Help or Heal
    by Dolores Krieger

Wheels of Life: A User's Guide to the Chakra System
    by Anodea Judith